LIVING WITH SEX: The Student's Dilemma

RICHARD F. HETTLINGER

THE
SEABURY
PRESS
New York

Library of Congress Catalog Card Number: 66-10835
Design by Nancy H. Dale
524-166-C-5
Printed in the United States of America

ACKNOWLEDGMENTS

See pages 181-182, which constitute an extension of this copyright page.

FOR THE KENYON COLLEGE CLASS
OF 1964: MY CONTEMPORARIES FOR FOUR DEMANDING
AND INSTRUCTIVE YEARS

PREFACE

The challenge to write about sex came during a four-year stint as chaplain to a liberal-arts college for men, and the basic argument was presented in a series of lectures to Kenyon students. The book is therefore addressed directly to men, but I believe it will be of interest to members of the other sex, as well as to precollege students, and to parents.

In the course of research and discussion, I became convinced that students are, contrary to popular opinion, at least as responsible in sexual matters as any group in our society. At the same time, they are the inheritors of an extremely confused and irrational moral code. They are not satisfied with the traditional religious approach to sex, nor with the libertarianism of many who have reacted against that approach. I have tried to clarify the nature of the dilemma, and to make clear what is involved in the various alternative solutions.

My own present view is that neither the negation of sex nor the unrestrained enjoyment of it is possible for the responsible, mature man. I have tried to show that this position is founded on solid facts and careful analysis, but conviction may well have led me to misinterpret or distort the evidence. If so, I am very ready to continue the debate on this urgent question with any who share my concern to do justice to the profundities and complexities of human existence.

R.F.H.

Kenyon College
October 22, 1965

CONTENTS

1 OUR DOUBLE-FACED SOCIETY

A friend of mine who is chaplain of a coeducational college in New England recently had a visit from a popular and attractive male student (who happened to be the son of a minister) with a lively reputation for sexual activity on the campus. Girls found him irresistible, and he was leaving a trail of broken hearts (and more) behind him. He admitted to the chaplain that his conduct was irresponsible and that he was concerned about his treatment of his consecutive bedmates; but he was honest enough to conclude, "The problem is, there's absolutely nothing I'd rather do at present than screw." Here, in a nutshell, is the student's dilemma. For what this young man was frank enough to admit is true of the great majority of male students—and of more of their seniors than would care to admit it. There was a great deal of truth as well as humor in the *Playboy* cartoon which showed a couple in bed together, obviously *post coitum,* and the girl asking, "Well, what *were* your second and third wishes?"

In our complex and competitive world, sexual needs and satisfactions are inextricably complicated by economic, moral, religious, and social factors which we do not control and which we cannot entirely ignore, however much we wish to. Sex is not in itself a "problem" but one of the fundamental facts of human existence; yet the adolescent grows up in a society which treats it as a problem. Indeed, our sexuality is debased and perverted to some degree. The tragedy is that we have come to think of sex itself as the problem, rather than the abuse and misunderstanding of sex. Sex—and by the word I mean the whole wonderful richness of relationship between men and women, not merely the physical or venereal pleasure which is only part of that relationship—can be among the most constructive, liberating, and enriching of human experiences. It can also be the most frustrating, destructive, and confusing of experiences. Most students know something of the fascination and excitement of confronting the mystery of human personality embodied in a member of the other sex. But for most of them, this meeting involves at one time or another anguish, remorse, disappointment, and despair. Not only do they somehow fail to be their best selves in this situation, but they are torn between the well-nigh insatiable demands of burgeoning physical potentialities and the frequently confused and contradictory ideals with which society presents them. Whether the student's tendency is to be traditionally moralistic, or violently rebellious like a Henry Miller, with his brilliant spoofing of conventional sexual standards, he cannot simply shed the inhibitions and restrictions imposed on him by parents, churches, and college administrations. Even less can he ignore the economic structure of our civilization. The best he can do, and the most that this book can help him to do, is to understand the facts, gain some perspective on the alternatives which are open to him, and then try to act with integrity.

Adult Ambivalence

The student's dilemma is exacerbated by, if it does not actually originate in, the ambivalent attitude of his elders toward their own sexuality. In matters of sexual behavior his natural and inevitable questioning of the traditional mores confronts no clear-cut practice in the adult world. He grows up in the context of a sort of public schizophrenia, in a society which is "sex-centric but sex rejecting." [1] To develop his own identity in the necessary adolescent revolt against the experience and stability of the established social order is difficult and painful enough for a young man (as his elders frequently forget); but to do so when there exists a gaping contradiction between what the social order officially says and what it continually practices becomes almost intolerable.

Instead of being able to engage in a dialogue with his parents, the contemporary student finds that his parents and their friends (without admitting it) are themselves in conflict with their own professed standards. And to have the privilege of revolt undercut by a secret alliance of worn-out adults is, to put it mildly, disturbing. Under the circumstances, it is not surprising that in a recent Gallup Poll, 37 per cent of the teenagers questioned blamed the laxity of their parents for the low standards of adolescent morality.[2] Even if they do not want to conform to parental standards, many students want them as a base for establishing their own standards; and they want them straight. But this they do not get. The sociologist Ashley Montagu has, on occasion, sharply underscored this contradiction.[3]

Parents encourage, or at least endorse, a system of dating which, from the age of prepuberty, utilizes all the traditional forms of elementary endearment and initial love-making in the game of casual relationships. Adolescents are pushed into adult situations far too early, often by mothers who want them to be well adjusted and who see in their children's popularity and "maturity" a substitute for the success they themselves failed to achieve. One result of this speeding-up of the dating process is that the currency of sexual encounter is debased. The couple who find themselves really in love, but unable immediately to marry, have run out of change to maintain and deepen their sexual relationship. Having exhausted every technique of kissing, necking, and petting in the minor leagues, there is nothing left to young people by which to mark steady dating or engagement other than going to bed together—a procedure which the adult generation promptly forbids or at least discourages. Gael Greene records the rather pathetic remark of a college girl who had pretty well covered the territory sexually:

> One thing, though. I really miss necking. Sex is so casual and taken for granted—I mean we go to dinner, we go home, get undressed like old married people, you know—and just go to bed. It's really like a marriage-type thing. I mean I'm not saying I'd like to be raped on the living room floor exactly. But I would love to just sit around on the sofa and neck.[4]

Of course, parents *qua* parents are by no means entirely to blame for the fact that the sexual desires of their offspring are consistently stimulated to a pitch which can only be adequately resolved in sexual intercourse. Adult society as a whole (of which parents form a good percentage) uses every possible form of visual sexual titillation to market its wares, and commercial interests thrive on worthless pornographic literature and crude "skin flicks." Television shows and movies take it for granted that the only possible reason for a man and a woman being together is to hop into bed; but when teenagers do what they have obviously been invited to do, society either punishes them or looks embarrassedly the other way.

A quick glance at the magazine rack or the paperback stand in almost any drug store will confirm that sex is one of the most lucrative commodities on the market today. Padded brassières are available to twelve-year-old girls. Teenage girls, who are now the chief target of the manufacturers' advertising, spend $25,000,000 a year on deodorants, $20,000,000 on lipstick, and $9,000,000 on home permanents.[5] We all know that boys buy a certain hair tonic not for the simple purpose of keeping their hair in order, but to exert a magical power over another fellow's girl. Dissatisfied customers even complain when they get a redhead instead of that slinky blonde who oozes out of the tube several times a week on millions of TV sets. And hardly anybody can be ignorant of the disastrous consequences of using more than one dab of the beastly stuff. Recently, a tobacco firm distributed a pack of samples which included a useful and informative little booklet on "the art [and advantages] of pipe smoking." The *text* of the booklet goes no further than to claim that the act of lighting up a pipe seems magically to endow a man with the attributes of "leadership, thoughtfulness, reliability, level-headedness—a long list of admirable characteristics which add up to a splendid masculine picture." But the illustrations suggest that this particular tobacco is also sexually potent by showing sexy girls eyeing the man hungrily as he fills and lights his pipe, beauties in bathing suits sitting, stretching, and kneeling in the bowl of the pipe, and finally a playful female figure cavorting in the smoke as he puffs away.

Now, I quote these examples not in order to start a campaign against girls in advertising or to enroll recruits in a legion of decency, but to illustrate the all-pervasive cultural pressure that establishes and maintains the centrality of sex in the thinking of young men. What is tragic is that the image conveys almost nothing of the complexity of sex and offers nothing in the way of guidance for its proper understanding. Despite the tremendous increase in the public representation of sex and the steady break-up of nineteenth-century standards of censorship, the twentieth century has done perhaps a worse job than any other in helping its youth to come to terms with this profoundly difficult subject. Phyllis and Eberhard Kronhausen, in their valuable study of the sexual experiences of two hundred male students, discovered that *scarcely one or two* had received anything even faintly resembling adequate sex education in the home or anywhere else.[6] Everyone knows that excellent books are readily available which explain the physical facts of sex,[7] but even with this kind of help, parents apparently find it emotionally impossible to discuss the matter with their children. Many of them still suffer from the inhibitions of one English woman, who, when asked by a social worker what she had done to give sex education to her son, replied that she had told him about most things, "even about girls and the monthlies, but I can't bring myself to tell him what his dad's for."

The Consequences of the Failure to Communicate

The consequences of this breakdown of communication between adults and adolescents may be far more serious than we sometimes realize. The fact that information about sex is, sooner or later, picked up from the peer group does not mean that the emotional attitude to this knowledge is what it would have been if the parental role had been adequately played. "In this process of 'education,' " write the Kronhausens, "many of the students had come to associate sex with the idea of sin and depravity, had lost further confidence in the integrity of their parents, and had . . . later experienced great difficulty in fusing affectionate and tender feelings with the lustful dynamics of the sexual impulse." [8]

It might be supposed that the widespread introduction of courses on sex education in the schools, since the nineteen-thirties, would have done something to compensate for the failure of parents. But this is not the case. The difficulties in providing suitable courses are considerable, and the educational experts are still greatly divided as to the best approach. Meanwhile, courses on "sexual hygiene" tend to fight shy of anything more explosive than the mating of the birds and the bees. And even this information is often so presented as to arouse prurient curiosity without in any way meeting the emotional and moral needs of the student. As Albert Ellis has pointed out:

> No one, for example, would begin to teach a child homemaking tasks and responsibilities by beginning: "The home is a sacred place and cooking and cleaning are beautiful God-given occupations which must always be carried out in a serious and sober manner so that the fundamental purposes of life may be gloriously fulfilled." Yet, this is the kind of hokum with which our books and talks on sex education are commonly filled. Naturally when handed this type of "enlightenment" the bright child quickly begins to wonder what it is about sex that is so intrinsically filthy that mealymouthed words by the dozen are needed to help clean it up.[9]

Even when a more enlightened school or teacher attempts to tackle the subject, local public opinion, which is, after all, made up largely of parents, who might have been expected to welcome some help, frequently clamps down. Paul Goodman, in *Growing Up Absurd,* recounts an incident in California in 1959 in which a high-school science teacher proposed to tabulate the class's sexual habits as an exercise in fact finding. The school board, in rebuking him, pointed out that he could only teach human reproduction in the same way as he discussed the functions of the eye or the ear. And Paul Goodman rightly comments that this is equivalent to teaching those subjects "without mentioning light or sound, color or harmony, or any other act or relation." [10]

The same failure to face up to the realities of adolescent sex needs and experience is reflected in the irrational public reaction to television treatment of the subject. Every kind of sadistic violence is readily accepted as part of the daily fare for children of all ages. The soap operas depict a steady sequence of petty infidelities, adulteries, divorces, and abortions. But when *The Defenders* put on a serious dramatic presentation of the problem of abortion, there was a howl of anguish. And when an attempt was made recently to present the dangers of teenage venereal disease in two popular series, the script was turned down. Despite the fact that the programs had the backing of the American Public Health Association and the Surgeon General of the United States, NBC rejected it because "it would have involved a discussion of sexual intercourse, which the network considered an unsuitable subject for television." [11] The action of NBC itself is rational enough, however ultimately irresponsible. Any public entertainment medium which puts popularity before principle (as 95 per cent of their shareholders demand) is bound to kowtow to the accepted convention that prefers to enjoy and use sex without ever facing up to its implications and complexities.

It may be helpful to remind ourselves that the failure of communication between adults and adolescents is not new in Western society. Lord Russell, who was dismissed from the City College of New York for his liberal views on marriage, complained nearly forty years ago that the gulf between the generations made it impossible for American parents to help their children with advice on sexual matters.[12]

But there is a difference. Whereas, in 1929 there was still a profound gap between the sexual practice of many parents and that of their children, so that the failure of communication may be in part explained as a lack of common experience, this is no longer true today. There is indeed still a gap between the professed public morality of the adult world and that of the teenager or college student. But there is surprisingly little difference between their respective sexual histories. I do not mean simply that current adult sexual license as reflected in the divorce courts and the successive polygamy of film stars conflicts with what society holds up to its youth as normative. That discrepancy might be explained, and sometimes is (however unconvincingly), as the privilege of middle age. But what the Kinsey reports have made clear is that, although today's student is undoubtedly more ready to boast about and defend his sexual emancipation, his father actually enjoyed—though more discreetly—a very similar sexual freedom. The precise forms of sexual outlet have changed. There is more petting to orgasm and less visiting of prostitutes today.

In the twenty years since Kinsey gathered the material for his book *Sexual Behavior in the Human Male,* there has certainly been an increase in the percentage of students engaging in intercourse. But the real change came with the generation born between 1900 and 1910, who were in their teens just after World War I. Since then, there has been a progressive trend toward justifying sexual freedom, or rather a progressive repudiation of the need to justify one's natural inclinations. The overt sexual behavior of today's student, the public and dramatic representation of sex, the language appropriate at polite cocktail parties—all approximate much more closely to what actually goes on in private or semiprivate. But the actual practice of this generation is very little different from that of those who graduated forty years ago. Kinsey found:

[The] increase in the incidence of premarital coitus, and the similar increase in the incidence of premarital petting, constitute the greatest changes which we have found between the patterns of sexual behavior in the older and younger generation of American females. . . . Practically all of this increase had occurred in the generation that was born in the first decade of the present century and, therefore, in the generation which had had most of its premarital experience in the late teens and in the 1920's following the First World War. The later generations appear to have accepted the new pattern and maintained or extended it.[13]

There was a great deal of truth in the cartoon which showed a father pacing the bedroom floor waiting for his daughter to say goodnight to her date in the car parked outside. His wife says to him, "Come to bed; can't you remember when you were young?" And he replies, "You bet; that's what I'm worried about."

The trouble is that self-knowledge is so painful to the senior generation that it cannot admit its own sexuality to its children and help them to face the issues squarely. The chances are that the father, in the cartoon waiting for his daughter, would put on a show at breakfast the next day, bemoaning the sensuality and profligacy of the young. If he were a judge, clergyman, politician, or educator, he would probably be happy to take any suitable opportunity to remind the world how much better behaved his generation was when it was young. His wife would be even more successful in drawing a total veil over her past and in holding up to her daughter (or her son) the lily-white ideal of what "nice" people do—or rather, don't do—before the marriage night. The assumption that mother never had anything to do with sex and lived in her virginity for twenty-five years untouched by the male does not, of course, prevent her children from engaging in illicit sexual practices. It only serves to ensure that their attitudes toward sexuality are distorted from the start.

Freud long ago pointed out the disastrous consequences of the tendency to divide women into two opposite classes—whores and angels. In his day this was not altogether surprising; but we might have expected that the present "emancipated" generation of mothers would have succeeded in overcoming the chasm. Studies show that in many cases the male student's difficulties over sex arise from or focus in his inability to associate physical sexuality and "pure" womanhood. He enjoys sex only with "bad" girls, but chooses a wife from those who conform to the ideal of sexual "purity" personified by his mother or sister —frequently with disastrous results after marriage.[14]

James Cartwright Holland, whose superbly funny contretemps with Kitten are recounted in Robert Gover's *One Hundred Dollar Misunderstanding,* put the point beautifully:

There are these two *un*professional ladies of ill repute I happen to know at home. One is Marg and the other is Susie. Despite their already ruined reputations I refuse to mention their last names. I'm not a cad, for gosh sakes! On the other hand, I'm not a prude either. What I mean to say is, I'm just a normal nineteen-year-old fellow, with normal appetites and all that, and these girls (at home) are always calling me up anyway. Don't get me wrong—I certainly don't go with either one of them. As previously mentioned, Barbara is my girl, and she's a very high-minded girl too. I wouldn't *touch* Barbara. I'm not that type. As a matter of fact, we may marry some day. But marriage, for me, and also for Barbara, is in the future, so as I've already mentioned, there are these two girls at home, whom I occasionally date. I mean, *go out with.* I can't really consider them *dates,* for gosh sakes!

Our Cultural Schizophrenia

Well, what is the explanation of this cultural schizophrenia, this failure on the part of the adult world to admit to its offspring or to itself that the traditional mores were abandoned in fact (though not in theory) decades before the present group of college students was born? I suggest that the adult generation has tried sexual freedom, enjoyed its first flush of blissful rapture, and discovered that the mystery of human relationships cannot be satisfied by promiscuity. There is no going back to the old assumptions, but our society has completely failed to develop any positive standards of sexual responsibility to take their place. Parents are unable to admit to their children that they, too, share and shared in sexual desire and experimentation, because they cannot offer any principles or conclusions to guide their children in the future. They are in near panic at the prospect of this generation reproducing and extending the trend toward promiscuity, for which they bear responsibility. They still enjoy their liberation from Victorian convention and yet are terrified at the emptiness of freedom without purpose, of lust without love, of independence without discipline. Quite unable to put the genie back into the bottle, our society, on the one hand, enjoys a vicarious second youth in its encouragement and stimulation of adolescent sexuality, and, on the other hand, attempts to relieve its sense of guilt and failure by imposing on the young those same conventional taboos from which it broke away.

The depths of the problem can be illustrated by the violent and irrational way in which adults react to those of their number who dare to call in question the absolute character of the accepted mores, which they see as the last bulwark (however widely breached) against chaos. So insecure and confused are our solons that any frank discussion of the realities of sexual behavior is impossible. In 1960, Professor Leo Koch, of the Department of Biology at the University of Illinois, was fired because he was rash enough to suggest in the campus paper that there is "no valid reason why sexual intercourse should not be condoned among those sufficiently mature to engage in it without violating their own codes of morality and ethics." [15] I have not read the full account of Koch's position, and I doubt whether I would agree with his solution to the problem. But his right to raise the question, particularly in view of the now-known facts of student sexual activity, I would defend. Certainly, the manner in which an opinion contrary to the public code was dealt with would, in the words of the ACLU statement at the time, "leave the young with the impression that conventional morality cannot stand the scrutiny of public discussion." [16]

Even more recently in England, a senior official of the British Ministry of Education caused a furor by telling a meeting of teachers: "I do not think it is wrong if a young man and woman who are in love and who intend to get married but who put off marriage, perhaps for economic reasons, have sexual intercourse before marriage. I do not think they are unchaste or immoral. They may or may not be wise if they do so, but I cannot convince myself that they are immoral." [17] The resultant uproar, including questions in the House of Commons, was the more noisy because Britain had just lived through the Profumo-Keeler scandal, and it was clearly felt to be essential to reaffirm absolute standards at any cost, however little resemblance they bear to the actual behavior of the populace.

The "problem" of sex, then, is at least as much an adult problem as a youth problem. Indeed, Lester A. Kirkendall has pointed out: "Nothing can be done until we as adults face facts in a realistic, frank, and objective way. The average adult is so ashamed of sex, and so fearful of the sexual impulse, that he is hampered and inhibited in any effort to be objective about sex. . . . The average adult has lost the capacity to acknowledge his own sexuality openly or refer to his own sexual needs and desires." [18] Until society comes to terms more effectively with the contradiction between its own practice and its official standards, it has no reason to complain if students fail to take them seriously.

2

THE STUDENT AS SCAPEGOAT

One dimension of the student's sexual dilemma has only been widely recognized since the publication of Kinsey's monumental *Sexual Behavior in the Human Male*—namely, the fact that men attain the greatest sexual capacity in their late teens.[1] Previously, it had been widely assumed that the maximum sexual potential was achieved in the middle twenties or later, and this theory fitted neatly into the assumptions of a social order which disapproved of premarital sexual intercourse and wished to delay both sexual activity and marriage. In a widely circulated book, published in 1879, Dr. J. H. Kellogg, a respected physician, made the following remarkable dogmatic assertion:

> Physiology fixes with accuracy the earliest period at which marriage is admissible. This period is that at which the body attains complete development, which is not before 20 in the female, and 24 in the male. Even though the growth may be completed before these ages, ossification of the bones is not fully effected, so that development is incomplete. . . . *If the body* [*of either parent*] *is still incomplete, the reproductive elements must also be incomplete;* and, in consequence, the progeny must be equally immature.[2]

But, on the contrary, Kinsey's studies showed that "teenage boys are potentially more capable and often more active than their 35-year-old fathers."[3] The student who finds living with sex a serious problem because his sexual desires refuse to be stilled by logic or cold baths is no monster, but a perfectly normal and healthy human being. Yet he grows up in a society which not only fails to acknowledge its own sexuality, but blames the younger generation for sexual nonconformity, which is almost inevitable in our culture and is frequently exaggerated and misrepresented.

Factors Complicating the Expression of Sexuality

In our culture the expression of sexuality is cabined and confined by a variety of complicating factors—some inseparable from our civilization, others entirely irrational, and most incomprehensible and frustrating to the growing man. The fulfillment of sexual relations in marriage is an economic impossibility for the great majority under twenty, particularly if they have any interest in higher education. On the other hand, religious sanctions and social conventions either morally condemn or legally prohibit all but one of the extramarital outlets (to use Kinsey's very clinical and rather unhappy term) for physical sexuality. Nocturnal seminal emissions, or "wet dreams," are the only means generally acceptable to conventional Western society by which the young man can obtain relief from the strain and pressure of sexual powers which, in another age, would have made him the father of a family. Some authorities have even contended that the frequency of wet dreams can, and should, be controlled by changing the position in sleep or choosing different night wear! [4]

Other means of outlet are condemned by laws drawn up by the older members of society, who have an uncanny capacity for forgetting their own adolescent sexual practices. Indeed, Kinsey estimated that 85 per cent of the younger male population could be convicted as sex offenders if law enforcement officials were as efficient as most adults expect them to be.[5] It is generally known that sexual intercourse outside of marriage is illicit and subject to penalty in most states of the Union. The couple can be fined $500 in Texas or jailed for three years in Arizona. What is not so widely known is that there are laws in several states forbidding many of the petting practices now commonly accepted by students if the girl is under twenty-one, *even if she consents*. Genital contact in heavy petting may bring a prison sentence of ten years in Indiana and Wyoming, of three in New Jersey, and of five in Michigan. Although there is no law which expressly forbids self-masturbation in private, the statutes of Indiana could be interpreted as prohibiting any sex instruction which "encourages" masturbation by correcting the popular misconceptions about its effects.[6] But what the laws do not expressly forbid is condemned as immoral and dangerous by female schoolteachers and celibate clergy, whose sexual needs, if not actually less, are obviously more amenable to restraint than those of the average student.

It is well known that Kinsey's researches showed that 85 per cent of the male population engages in premarital intercourse, and more than 95 per cent admits to one or other of the means of sexual relief which are officially taboo in our society.[7] Since a very small percentage are prosecuted for these activities, it is obvious that the laws attempting to govern sexual activity are unenforced and generally unenforceable. Certainly, they are not taken seriously by students. The traditional public standards represented by the legal codes and the protestations of official spokesmen for the Establishment are simply ignored or ridiculed by men (and women) in college. Nevertheless, the continued existence and occasional implementation of such expressions of public condemnation reflect the widespread failure of the adult world to come to terms with, and to give adequate guidance to, the sexual needs of adolescence and early manhood. Indeed, I would go further and agree with Colin MacInnes that the older generation have "an almost obscene obsession with the sexuality of the young . . . prompted by envious rancour and a bullying intention to interfere." [8] It is characteristic that those who are too old to dance the frug, the jerk, or the monkey frequently deplore the vulgarity and "sexiness" of these dances, and remind their children of the languid and graceful pirouettes of the past. It may be some help to point out that it was always so. Havelock Ellis, in his still-classic study, *The Psychology of Sex,* discusses the current question of the "wholesomeness" of the "new" dances, and refers to an article entitled "The Psychopathology of the New Dances," by A. A. Brill, which showed that they were not, in fact, "gross sexual inciters." [9] And the date of Brill's study? 1914!

It is, of course, the college student and particularly the male student who epitomizes for the general public the breakdown of sexual morality. The first newsletter of the recently established Sex Information and Education Council of the United States (SIECUS) set forth as its excellent aim "to establish man's sexuality as a health entity . . . , to dignify it by openness of approach, study and scientific research designed to lead toward its understanding and its freedom from exploitation." [10] The Council then went on to express concern over the failure of much current discussion to get at the real issues involved, and pointed out that "favorite scapegoats are the college students whose widely publicized behavior has given rise to an epidemic of tongue-clucking among adults, all of whom are beyond college age." Now, I am not about to deny that a great deal of irresponsible sexual activity occurs on every campus. But there are a number of facts which bear on this public image and need to be emphasized if we are to have anything like an adequate picture of the sexual dilemma of the student.

What Are the Facts?

In the first place, Kinsey found that whereas about 70 per cent of the total male population engaged in coitus at least occasionally between the ages of sixteen and twenty-five, the corresponding figure for males who go beyond the twelfth grade was only 48 per cent—about one-third less.[11] Undoubtedly, both these figures have increased since Kinsey did his research, and it is likely that the gap between the educational levels has narrowed: the upper educational level has unquestionably been more influenced by the revelations of Kinsey's own work than the lower educational groups. Dr. Graham B. Blaine, Jr., the student-health-service psychiatrist at Harvard, now estimates the percentage of male students engaging in intercourse before graduation at 60 per cent.[12] Be that as it may, some of Kinsey's comments on the discrepancy between college students and other young men are still highly relevant. He pointed out: "The mother who is afraid to send her boy away to college for fear that he will be morally corrupted there, is evidently unaware of the histories of the boys who stay at home. Moreover, nearly half of the males who have intercourse while in college had their first experience while they were still at home, before they started to college." [13] Furthermore, the college student is likely, if he does have intercourse before marriage, to engage in it far less frequently and with fewer companions than his contemporaries in the lower educational groups. Despite the widespread boasting on the subject, students are far less likely ever to visit a prostitute than men whose education concluded in grade or high school. Kinsey found that only about one college graduate in four, even of those who are still unmarried at twenty-five, had ever had this experience.[14] And he points out that a good many college males "never have premarital intercourse with more than the one girl whom they subsequently marry, and very few of them have premarital intercourse with more than half a dozen girls or so." [15]

There are two questions worth pursuing. Why do college students have such an undeserved reputation for excess? And why are they, in fact, less promiscuous than their less educated contemporaries? Undoubtedly, the reputation is due in part to the descriptive imagination of the student, who for reasons of prestige or pure egoism translates his intentions and desires into actuality for the benefit of fraternity members or the kids back home. One of Kinsey's most striking conclusions was: "An upper level male who is not married thinks of sex as masturbation, nocturnal emissions, petting, and *a continual excitement over girls with whom he would like relations, but with whom he rarely effects actual coitus.*" [16] The brilliant satirical review *The Committee* has a very effective sketch, "Sex on Campus," which illustrates this point. A boy is showing his girl round the fraternity house and invites her to view the bedroom. She demurs because she says she doesn't love him. He replies that that doesn't worry him at all, and begs her to go to bed with him. Eventually, he has to be satisfied with a kiss. Yet, when the girl has gone, and his roommate asks, "Did you score?" he replies gaily, "Of course; don't I always?"[17] A second element contributing to the impression of sexual promiscuity among students is the practice of heavy petting, frequently in public or semipublic places. Kinsey found that among the lower educational groups, manual genital stimulation was widely regarded as a sign of perversion, whereas it is often accepted among college students as a substitute for actual coitus.[18] The general population, observing the activities of students, concludes that they are not only "oversexed" but that they find relief in undesirable and obscene practices. Yet many students believe that by avoiding the act of penetration, they have preserved their virginity. Whether they are justified in this assumption is a matter for later consideration, but the practice obviously contributes to the popular picture of the student as a rake.

The reasons underlying the student's relative sexual restraint are varied and complex. Undoubtedly, the economic factor enters into the picture. The student knows that an accident leading to forced marriage, or the development of a relationship in which early marriage becomes inevitable, would very likely put an end to his academic career. Again, the whole cultural pattern of sexual relationships in the upper educational levels requires more romantic preliminaries to intercourse, which are both time consuming and expensive. It is striking that, in contrast to many men of lesser education, students almost unanimously report that experiences with prostitutes are humiliating, unsatisfying, or revolting because the arrangement "lacks the affection which makes a sexual relation significant."[19]

The college student is also far more deeply imbued with the distinctive Jewish-Christian respect for virginity than he would like to admit. He usually breaks with the tradition of church or synagogue attendance as soon as he arrives on campus. He readily questions the theological ideas associated with his family faith. He publicly dissociates himself from the antisexuality of much church teaching. But he finds it far less easy in practice to free himself from ingrained assumptions about sexual practice. Whether one regards the traditional mores as beneficial, disastrous, or (as I do) partly one and partly the other, their continued influence upon students must be recognized.

Among those males between sixteen and twenty-five in the upper educational level in Kinsey's sample who regarded themselves as active or devout Christians (a surprisingly high 43 per cent), premarital intercourse was only half as common as among the nonactive Protestants and Catholics of the same age and educational level.[20] The reasons given for abstaining from intercourse by these young men would not usually be those given by their churches; but the continuing impact of traditional standards cannot be ignored. Kinsey attempted to minimize the significance of these figures because, as he pointed out, the divergences between upper and lower educational groups *within* the churches are greater than the differences of practice between the nonchurchman and the churchman in each educational group.[21] Although this should certainly give the ecclesiastical authorities food for thought, it is not decisive. Kinsey's point is equivalent to saying that, for example, the differences between the living standards of American Negroes and American whites are insignificant because there happens to be an even greater difference between the living standards of Americans and Africans. The fact remains that among educated young men the influence of religious tradition on sexual standards is considerable, and more so than among the less well educated.

Finally, we must recognize that it is not only the student with a strong religious background for whom moral standards remain significant. *Newsweek,* in its article "The Morals Revolution on the U.S. Campus" noted that "while today's students may convince themselves intellectually that sex is good, they seem to feel almost as guilty about sex for sex's sake as did their predecessors." [22] The fact is that the student is not simply engaged in a blind rejection of societal mores; he is looking for a more honest and rational approach to sex which will help him to make sense of it. He is entirely dissatisfied with, and unconvinced by, the pat black-and-white distinctions that parents, teachers, and clergy have handed out to him. He is disillusioned by the hypocrisy of the society in which he is growing up. But he is not generally irresponsible, perverse, or promiscuous. He senses, however inadequately, the mystery and dangers of sex as well as its delights. He wants to develop satisfying interpersonal relationships. He is, above all, possessed by an exhilarating, threatening, overwhelming need to express his sexuality; and he is confronted by laws and prohibitions and taboos which attempt, however unsuccessfully, to prevent that expression. He is confused rather than degenerate, the victim of society's dishonesty rather than a proper scapegoat for its justification. Above all, he is ready to listen if anyone will offer him intelligible and realistic values which will lift the veil of bigotry and prudery from the subject and help him to appreciate the depths and beauty of sexual relationships. That, alas, is exactly what the religious traditions do not offer him.

3 THE IRRELEVANCE OF RELIGION

In most ages other than our own, the title of this chapter would have involved almost a direct contradiction in terms. For, as B. Z. Goldberg illustrates in his somewhat sensational and speculative work, *The Sacred Fire: The Story of Sex in Religion,* the great majority of religions have utilized the sexual instinct as an expression of man's deepest being.[1] The obvious parallel between human fertility and the food-bearing role of Mother Earth, upon which men depend so decisively for their existence, has from very early times suggested a connection between sex and divinity, between ecstasy and worship. The earliest-known female figure was sculptured (perhaps for religious purposes) 20,000 years ago.[2] The perpetuation of thinly disguised sexual symbolism in the art and literature of religions that in theory repudiate or spiritualize sex shows how deeply rooted this association is. Goldberg's thesis that primitive religion originated in man's sexuality, though hardly proven, deserves further serious study. He argues that for man, as distinct from the earlier animals, "even when love was a brief, physical, sex hunger, it embodied something more. . . . Promiscuous as the original sex life of man was, cruelly and brutally as it may have expressed itself, it still contained the trace of an attitude toward the objective of his desire. There was no suggestion of such an attitude toward the meat that stilled his hunger, or the water that quenched his thirst." [3] Whether the religious attitude originated in the experience of sex or not, most human cultures have recognized their close connection.

In Western culture the relevance of religion to sex was also taken for granted until recently, but here the influence has been largely negative and restrictive. The American consciousness is deeply scarred by the oppressive influence of Puritanism—

so much so that the positive contributions of that tradition to our society are almost entirely forgotten except on Thanksgiving Day. On all other occasions the term carries such pejorative associations that to label one's opponent or critic as a "Puritan" is enough to render any serious examination of his argument unnecessary. "The value we have given to that word," wrote the demon Screwtape in C. S. Lewis's *Screwtape Letters,* "is one of the really solid triumphs of the last hundred years. By it we rescue annually thousands of humans from temperance, chastity, and sobriety of life." [4] Recently, *Playboy* has provided us with the word "neopuritan" as an instrument of derision with which to dismiss any attempt at reformulating religious moral standards, however liberal.[5] Actually, the Puritans didn't invent prudery. It was Pope Paul IV who had the nudes in Michelangelo's Last Judgment provided with panties, and Pope Innocent X who had a shirt painted on the naked baby Jesus.[6] Indeed, in recent times it has been the Roman Catholics, rather than the successors of the Puritans, who have been most hesitant about accepting the sexual revolution. But any stick is good enough to beat a dog with, and the term "Puritan" effectively reflects the popular, and understandable, impression that religion identifies the body with evil and sexual pleasure with sin. And for this reason, religion, even as a negative force, has widely ceased to be relevant to the life of modern man. Although students are more influenced by traditional inhibitions than their less educated contemporaries, religious *arguments* carry little weight with them.

How Irrelevant Is Religion?

As we noted in the previous chapter, Kinsey discovered that premarital intercourse was only half as common among college-level men between sixteen and twenty-five who described themselves as "devout" or "active" Christians as among the non-active.[7] The total sexual outlets of the religiously devout he found to be only two-thirds those of the religiously inactive, though he hazarded the guess that "some portion of the devoutly religious individuals have repressed rather than sublimated sex histories." [8]

If we look at the actual figures in Kinsey's Protestant sample, however, it is obvious that the teaching of Protestant churches has little relevance to the sexual lives of most students. Nearly half of all the Protestants in the college-level group interviewed *twenty years ago* admitted that they had disregarded the most consistently proclaimed and explicit moral prohibition of their churches—that against extramarital sexual intercourse.[9] It is certain that this proportion has increased considerably since Kinsey's work was undertaken. Even more significant is the fact that, as Kinsey found and my personal knowledge of male students strongly confirms, those who refrain from intercourse do so either because they cannot bring themselves to set aside deep-seated inhibitions for which they have no conscious justification, or for reasons which are entirely different from those traditionally used to support chastity. I myself have found very few, even among the most regular churchgoers, who regard the teaching of their church or the Bible as relevant to their sexual activity. They refrain from intercourse not because the act is religiously condemned, but because they feel it to be too "precious" to engage in with anyone other than a marriage partner, or out of respect for the girl they are dating.

Equally, according to Kinsey, some girls who gave "moral" objections to premarital intercourse "insisted that they were not accepting the traditional codes just because they were the codes, and believed that they had developed their attitudes as a result of their own rational analyses of what they considered to be expedient, decent, respectable, fine, sensible, right or wrong, better or best." [10]

I do not in any way wish to knock a good thing (as the girl in one of *The Committee* sketches remarks when her roommate argues for virginity). I do not at all assent to the unexamined assumption that because the traditional sexual mores are only observed by the minority, their validity has been finally disproved. To a great extent it is not that Christianity has been tried and found wanting, but, in G. K. Chesterton's famous *mot,* that it has been found difficult and not tried. Nevertheless, I am convinced that the approach to sex which starts from authoritative codes and claims to have received a revelation that settles all the problems for man's sexual life is increasingly irrelevant to the needs of the majority of students, Christian or otherwise. Most of them can no longer live by "the rules of a long-gone game." [11]

The widespread failure to accept traditional Christian moral teaching, even among those who otherwise accept its doctrines, is not difficult to understand. The early prophets of sexual freedom had suffered under Victorian prudery, which claimed the sanctions of religion for its negative attitude toward all sexuality. St. Paul's unhappy dictum, "It is better to marry than to burn," is almost the only biblical text with which many writers on sex are acquainted, to judge from their use of it (almost invariably out of context and without any understanding of the background of the saying).[12] Every book extolling the joys of free love includes a chapter of horror stories about the perversions of the early church fathers and the sexual implications of witchcraft.[13]

Much of this literature exaggerates isolated events and unrepresentative opinions, taking St. Jerome as typical of all patristic thought or the Cathari as official voices of the medieval church. All too often it disregards one of the fundamental canons of historical research and estimates the significance of early Christian pronouncements not against the background of Roman dissolution or barbarian licentiousness, but against modern European cultural norms.[14] Yet, granted all this, the history of Christianity does show a prevailing tendency to regard physical sexuality as at best permissible and at worst demonic. Dr. Sherwin Bailey, who can hardly be suspected of prejudice in this respect since he is a clergyman, sums up his account of *Sexual Relation in Christian Thought* in these terms:

Almost from the beginning, we discern a markedly negative reaction to everything venereal which has profoundly and adversely affected the character and development of Christian sexual ideas—a reaction expressed with every degree of intensity from mild suspicion or apathy to violent hostility or revulsion. . . . The conviction rapidly gained ground, and became firmly entrenched in the early Church, that coitus is not only in some indefinable sense unclean and defiling, but also intrinsically evil or sinful, either on account of the concupiscence by which men and women are supposedly impelled thereto, or because of the sensual pleasure involved in the act.[15]

Sex and Sin

However much the Bible may have affirmed the goodness of God's creation, however significant St. Paul's analogy between sexual intercourse and Christ's union with his church,[16] however sensual the imagery of the mystics, the church has succeeded in leaving its members with the unavoidable impression that sex is a regrettable necessity, and sexual sin the worst of all evils. St. Augustine denied that the sex act originally and properly involved any emotional desire, and developed the doctrine of original sin in such a manner as virtually to equate it with sexual pleasure.[17] It is remarkable how much of the tradition of sexual ethics in our culture has been elaborated by celibate monks who were either less highly sexed than the average man, or, having sown their wild oats as pagans and having on conversion foresworn their youthful lusts, then proceeded in later life to enforce more rigid standards on the next generation.

Nothing has done more to confirm the impression that sex is intrinsically undesirable than the elevation of celibacy and virginity above marriage as not only a different but a higher Christian vocation. One sign of the distorted view to which we are heirs is the fact that when we speak of "living in sin," we never mean "living in pride" or "practicing segregation." Why is it that the word "immoral" immediately implies sexual deviation, never unfair business practice or the exploitation of labor? While concentrating its attention on sexual deviation, the church has often failed to speak out against the other evils of society. A number of years ago, Dorothy Sayers gave a brilliant lecture called *The Other Six Deadly Sins* to the Public Morality Council in London. She began thus:

> Perhaps the bitterest commentary on the way in which Christian doctrine has been taught in the last few centuries is the fact that to the majority of people the word "immorality" has come to mean one thing and one thing only. The name of an association like yours is generally held to imply that you are concerned to correct only one sin out of those seven which the Church recognizes as capital. By a hideous irony, our shrinking reprobation of that sin has made us too delicate so much as to name it, so that we have come to use for it the words which were made to cover the whole range of human corruption. A man may be greedy and selfish; spiteful, cruel, jealous and unjust; violent and brutal; grasping, unscrupulous and a liar; stubborn and arrogant; stupid, morose and dead to every noble instinct—and still we are ready to say of him that he is not an immoral man.[18]

There are, of course, signs of a reaction against this distortion in ecclesiastical circles; but it will be many decades before the heritage of antisexualism is erased from the image of the church. Under the circumstances it is not surprising that the student, to whom sex is among the most exciting potentialities of life, regards the official codes of Christendom as meaningless.

The Church and Marriage

Perhaps the fundamental reason for the church's irrelevance is the fact that religious teaching on sex has been almost entirely limited to the discussion of marriage. In a recent symposium, *Sex Ways in Fact and Faith,*[19] for example, the only references in the chapter "What Churches Say Today," by John C. Wynn, were to marriage and the family—with the single and significant exception of a phrase in a statement made in 1954 by two Lutheran churches which stated flatly, "Sex relations outside of marriage, whether before an intended marriage or outside an established bond, are a violation of God's will." [20] When Canon V. A. Demant delivered his very informative lectures, *Christian Sex Ethics,* to an undergraduate audience at Oxford University in 1963, he had virtually nothing whatever to say about sexual relations outside marriage. But there is very little help for the young man caught up in the crisis of adolescent sexuality today in telling him how highly the church values sex within marriage. Demant reminds us that the defense of marriage by early church fathers like Augustine was in marked contrast to the teaching of non-Christian cults such as the Gnostics and Manichaeans, who repudiated even this degree of sexuality.[21] Indeed, even within marriage the church has been, until recently, extremely grudging in its acceptance of physical sexuality. Augustine regarded marriage as primarily a sacramental means of forgiveness for the inevitable sin involved in the pleasure of coitus. Since the continuance of the race is necessary until God has made up the number of his elect, procreation is an unavoidable duty. Before the Fall, according to Augustine, it could have been achieved without the violent, irrational, physical pleasure of orgasm (a sheer impossibility in the light of modern knowledge of the physiology of sex). After the Fall, owing to man's depraved condition, a husband and wife are unable to conceive without some concupiscence and enjoyment; but within marriage the consequences of sin are not imputed penally when the couple have intercourse with the intention of procreating and not for pleasure.[22] In other words, even marriage only provides an *excuse* for sexual activity, which is still, insofar as it involves emotional and physical pleasure, evil.

Later discussions of marriage went beyond this purely negative and forensic view, and the Schoolmen recognized marriage as involving a contract for mutual comfort and help, as well as being the means of reproduction. Even here, however, there is little understanding of coitus itself as a vital expression of love between husband and wife. The couple benefit from each other in many ways—in the common provision of food and home, in sickness, in spiritual encouragement, in the raising of children. But the act of sexual intercourse remains suspect—a distasteful obligation to be gone through with regret and all possible objectivity. St. Thomas Aquinas argued that wedlock without carnal intercourse is really more holy, and he and other Schoolmen quoted with approval the saying of the philosopher Xystus: "He who loves his own wife too ardently is an adulterer." [23] Some medieval moralists recommended abstinence from coitus on fast days and certain festivals, on Thursday in memory of Christ's arrest, on Friday in memory of his death, on Saturday in honor of the Virgin Mary, and on Monday in commemoration of the departed. Had these regulations been generally acted upon, Western society must perforce have come to an end for lack of progeny! I am reminded of the statement about the Abelites in the *Encyclopedia Americana:* "An African sect which opposed procreation on the ground that it was a perpetuation of sin. Extinct." [24]

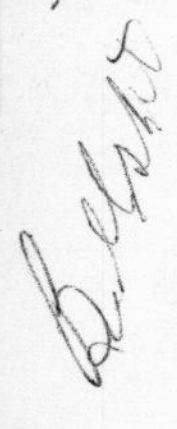

Nor is there much change in the attitude of the Reformers in this respect. Luther, of course, repudiated the double standard which set virginity above marriage as a state of grace; but he still regarded coitus as "a regrettable but imperative necessity," [25] and (since, like St. Paul, he expected the end of the world at any moment) justified marriage primarily not as the means of providing for children but as a cure for immorality. Calvin had a more wholesome appreciation of sexual union and a higher view of the marriage relationship as a bond in which the woman shares the man's whole life, not merely his bed. But he considered it inexcusable for a wife to touch that part of her husband's body "from the sight and touch of which all chaste women naturally recoil." Indeed, Sherwin Bailey believes that the first explicit acknowledgment among churchmen of the relational value of coitus is in the writing of the seventeenth-century Anglican Jeremy Taylor, who taught that intercourse was hallowed by the intention "to lighten and ease the cares and sadnesses of household affairs, or to endear each other" as well as for procreation and the avoidance of fornication.[26]

Romantic Love and Christian Marriage

By the seventeenth century, of course, the ideal of courtly, or romantic, love had affected orthodox Christian thinking about marriage. Through their romantic appreciation of sexual passion, the troubadours of the eleventh century, in the words of C. S. Lewis, "effected a change which has left no corner of our ethics, our imagination, or our daily life untouched, and they erected impassable barriers between us and the classical past or the Oriental present." [27] The original significance of this idealization of love, to which our present attitude toward sex is so largely indebted, remains a matter of considerable controversy; but what is certain is that the church at first regarded romantic love as a threat to its view of marriage.[28] This was partly for the understandable reason that the objects of amorous affection were always the wives of other men, and partly because the new ideal was confused with purely animal passion. Boccaccio's famous *Decameron* utilized the theme of courtly love in the interests of a sensual and largely selfish sexual code, which was essentially anti-Christian.[29] Nevertheless, by the end of the fourteenth century, romantic love had been quietly baptized and was accepted as right and desirable within marriage.[30] In the sixteenth century, Edmund Spenser could brilliantly portray sexual love as an element in the human expression of the creative, harmonizing, and sovereign power of the universe. To those who still found the earthiness of such passion religiously unacceptable, he replied:

Such ones ill iudge of loue, that cannot loue,
Ne in their frosen hearts feele kindly flame:
For thy [i.e., therefore] they ought not thing vnknowne reproue,

Ne naturall affection faultlesse blame,
For fault of few that haue abused the same.
For it of honor and all vertue is
The roote, and brings forth glorious flowres of fame,
That crowne true louers with immortall blis,
The meed of them that loue, and do not liue amisse.[31]

Whatever its limitations, romantic love did represent a view of life centered on another person, rather than on the self. It profoundly affected the status of women. And it introduced into sexual relationships a new understanding of the wholeness of human nature, which earlier church teaching had obscured. Yet the church never really freed itself of the heritage of medieval dualism. Victorian society reacted against the excesses of eighteenth-century sexuality, and with vigorous support from the pulpit, once again made any honest acceptance of sex impossible. It has been only within the last two or three decades that Christian thinkers, under the pressure of Freud's insights, have been forced to face the full implications of the biblical doctrine that God made man and woman in his own image and saw that it was good.[32] One of the earliest formal ecclesiastical affirmations of the positive value of sex appeared in the report of the Lambeth Conference of Anglican Bishops in 1930. This report recognized that the functions of sex "as a God-given factor in human life are essentially noble and creative," and spoke of coitus as a means whereby "married love is enhanced and its character strengthened." [33]

Some ten years ago, Canon H. C. Warner, at that time Education Secretary of the Church of England Moral Welfare Council, suggested the following at an ecumenical conference:

Traditional Catholic theology has not always given enough weight to the relational function of coitus, probably because most of those who fashioned medieval doctrine had no personal experience of this function within marriage. Its importance, however, can hardly be overstated. It is the moment of mutual orgasm which brings to its climax the *unitive experience* of coitus. In the woman there is a small organ, the clitoris, which has no other function than that of sensation directed to orgasm. In the light of the Christian doctrine of creation, the significance of this organ in the divine ordinance must not be overlooked, especially in assessing the unitive purpose of coitus.[34]

Even Roman Catholic thinking on this subject has been undergoing a transformation, as the current discussion on birth control indicates. It is one thing to argue, as the Roman Church has in the past, that the pleasures of intercourse are a concession to the flesh which are justified if the risk of conception is accepted, and quite another thing to recognize them as beneficial in themselves when the intention is to *avoid* procreation in the particular act. When Roman Catholic bishops propose to set up research centers to make possible the more effective use of the rhythm method for the enjoyment of intercourse without the danger of conception, the distinction between "natural" and "artificial" means of contraception seems to have been rendered absurd.[35] A totally new recognition of the value of sexuality within marriage is reflected in a recent study, *Contraception and Holiness: The Catholic Predicament,* edited by Archbishop Thomas D. Roberts. In this book a Catholic lay woman, Rosemary Ruether, writes:

The married person has sublimated the sexual drive into a *relationship* with another person. The sexual drive, for him, ceases to have any meaning or urgency simply as an egotistic drive, or self-centered bodily appetite. It is rather the intimate expression of one's relationship with this particular other person, this unique and irreplaceable other person. . . . Essentially the rhythm method is debilitating because it imposes an abnormal regime on the expression of marital love. It treats marital love as an appetite which can be scheduled, like eating and sleeping. But marital love, if it is really developed, has been sublimated from the appetite level.[36]

All this is to the good; but I fear it is still too late to overcome, within this generation, the deeply grounded suspicion that the churches regard physical sex even within marriage as essentially selfish, degrading, and irreligious. Moreover, it still entirely overlooks one inevitable complication. When marriage was regarded as a contract between two people for their mutual fellowship and the procreation of children, it was possible, at least in theory, to set the wedding day as the occasion on which sexual relations could begin. But once the concept of romantic love has been accepted as a valid and important element in the relationship of the sexes, it is no longer feasible to argue that all sexual intimacy must begin on a certain calendar date. A couple cannot be expected to fall in love just because they have been united in marriage; but, if we encourage young men and women to fall in love (as not only our culture but our churches do today) and regard this condition as a desirable qualification for marriage, we cannot ignore the problems raised by the fact that such love is essentially and unavoidably sexual from the start.

The Implications of Romantic Love

Of course, the religious authorities have recognized the problem; but their reactions to it have remained to date largely negative and prohibitive. There is very little indication that the churches have faced the fact that you cannot welcome sexual pleasure between married adults and still condemn it wholesale between unmarried adolescents. The dean of a Cambridge college, himself an ordained clergyman, has summed up the picture in a recent lecture:

> It is a sad but uncontrovertible fact that the Church has often . . . betrayed its ethical insight in the interests of a tidy moralistic respectability. It has sometimes dealt with sexual problems as though they could be settled and resolved by black and white rules. It has appeared more censorious than compassionate. And, in so doing, it has been infected by that kind of pharisaic hypocrisy which is the ultimate betrayal of Christian or of any moral life.[37]

The Kronhausens reflected a widespread and understandable impression when they wrote, "Neither in the precepts of Christian ethics, nor in the legal philosophy of the Western world, do we find any indication that the presence or absence of *love* should determine whether a given sexual act is to be considered right or wrong." [38]

The impression is, in fact, inaccurate because there is a growing body of opinion among theologians that affirms precisely the view that love should have precedence over law. *Time* magazine reported, on March 5, 1965, a meeting of 900 clergymen and students at the Harvard Divinity School to consider the so-called new morality: "an ethic based on love rather than law, in which the ultimate criterion for right and wrong is not divine command but the individual's subjective perception of what is good for himself and his neighbor in each given situation." [39] Nevertheless, this revolution is far from acceptance by many ecclesiastical authorities, and like the other belated concessions to humanity and reality described in this chapter, it will hardly arrive in high places in time to rescue the image of religion in the eyes of this student generation.

It is true that any society—religious or secular—has the difficult task of setting common standards and, in some circumstances, of penalizing its members when they fall below the accepted level. But all too often the church has failed to acknowledge even the possibility that the suspension of the norm or ideal *in sexual conduct* may, in certain cases, find ethical justification in the conscience of the individual. As Bishop Robinson has pointed out, this intransigence and rigidity has been distinctively characteristic of sexual ethics.[40] In many other areas, such as social theory and capital punishment, Christian thinking has adapted itself to different conditions and new knowledge; only in sexual questions is it generally assumed that some things are always right and others always wrong. Those who quote scripture to show that adultery is unforgivable or that homosexuals cannot share in the Kingdom of God find it quite possible to reinterpret Jesus' saying about turning the other cheek or his warning about the difficulty of the rich entering the Kingdom. In particular, as Bishop Robinson notes,

the application of the term "fornication" without qualification to all cases of sexual intercourse before marriage totally disregards the revolution involved in the acceptance of romantic love as a proper element in sexual relationships:

> To settle what is a responsible and searching question by a sweeping reference to "fornication and all uncleanness" (Eph. 5:3) is to invite the recent comment of an atheist that these questions are too serious to be discussed at the religious level. For *porneia,* as its derivation implies, always has associations in the New Testament with promiscuity, if not with prostitution. . . . To assume that this applies to all relationships between engaged couples is to prejudge the moral issue in an utterly insensitive and irresponsible way.[41]

But the moral theologians have shown just such an unhealthy tendency to extend the rule of law into areas where only personal judgment and integrity can make the final decision about what is good and right. Kinsey, for example, collected a fascinating but entirely depressing compendium of Catholic codes governing petting practices which he summarized as follows: "All sexual pleasure, complete or incomplete, can be lawfully desired or deliberately enjoyed only in marriage. Chaste touches are permitted to engaged couples if for pleasure of sensation, but not for venereal pleasure. Petting in marriage likewise may not be for pleasure, but only as leading to coitus or as a sign of mutual love."[42] A contemporary Protestant authority advises us with a straight face, "Before marriage it is best to keep every sort of sexual excitement toward your fiancée under complete control, since it is not good for her."[43] The student who comes across such pronouncements is likely to conclude that religious leaders have lost all touch with reality, or that words have ceased to have any meaning. And he will certainly look elsewhere for the guidance he desperately needs—probably to *Playboy.*

4

THE PLAYBOY PHILOSOPHY

"Playboy is more than just a handbook for the young-man-about-town: it's a sort of Bible which defines his values, shapes his personality, sets his goals, dictates his choices and governs his decisions. The *Playboy* philosophy has become . . . a sort of substitute religion." This judgment, by a writer in *Motive,*[1] was underscored for me by the comment of a friend who read the original lectures on which this book is based: "Don't make so much of Kinsey," he urged. "Kinsey's dead. What really counts in student discussions of sex today is *Playboy*." I pointed out that Hugh Hefner makes extensive use of the Kinsey findings, even on occasion devoting a whole installment of *The Playboy Philosophy* to quotes from *Sexual Behavior in the Human Male* (or *Female*); but my friend's point is well taken. Kinsey's figures are, relatively, objective and scientific. *Playboy* gives them flesh (almost literally) and interprets and adapts this new knowledge of sexual behavior to the immediate interest of the student. At last reporting, nearly a million copies of *Playboy* were being sold to men between eighteen and twenty-four, and probably six million people in this age group alone read (or at least see) the magazine every month.[2]

The popularity of *Playboy* among students is not difficult to understand in the light of the situation described in the previous chapters. Here is a well-produced magazine which treats the subject of sex with something like the degree of attention it occupies in the thinking of most young men, neither denying its reality as official society tries to do and questioning its value as the church does, nor isolating it from other interests as the cheap "girlie" magazines do. To describe *Playboy* as an academic critic did as "the whole man reduced to his private parts" tells us more about the author than about the magazine. It includes stories, articles, and interviews of first-class quality on a wide range of subjects from hypnosis to automobiles by internationally respected authors.

In contrast to many other "magazines for men," *Playboy* presents sex as a part of the whole man's concern in life rather than as his sole obsession. Furthermore, it includes an attempt to discuss the issues of our day in *The Playboy Philosophy*, which claims to offer a relevant sexual morality to fill the vacuum left by society and the church. Despite the repetitive and meandering character of this editorial, it is, to judge from the letters in the "Playboy Forum," read carefully and widely by people of very different backgrounds. Indeed, it has been reported that the smart thing to do on campus is to read the editorials and ignore the playmate of the month.[3] Hefner's ability as a writer and controversialist is obvious and attractive. For example, his discussion of the dismal history of the American rejection of Charlie Chaplin showed great insight,[4] and it was clear from his part in the round-table radio discussion on sex that he can defend his position with vigor and sincerity—though not, I think, with complete success.[5]

A Much-Needed Protest

Much of Hefner's concern, and much of his success, lies in poking fun at the sacred cows and outdated taboos of our double-faced society. Undoubtedly, the various attempts by the Chicago authorities to squash him have been due to his criticism of the establishment and his persistent and well-documented revelation of the fact that the emperor (like the girls in the magazine) has no (or very few) clothes. He shows up the absurdities of our antiquated and inconsistent sex laws,[6] decries the persecution of the unfortunate Lenny Bruce, and very properly and rightly denounces the vigilante tactics of such self-appointed guardians of the public morality as the National Organization for Decent Literature.[7]

Some of Hefner's illustrations of the workings or misworkings of the state and local obscenity laws are hilarious. The head of Atlanta's five-member movie-censorship board, a housewife, explained on a TV interview that *Never on Sunday* had been banned because it included the word "whore." Other films with a similar theme had been admitted but, "We've called them *tramps;* we've called them *ladies of easy virtue;* we've called them *call girls;* we've called them . . . *girls of the night;* but ['whore'] is a word that we have not customarily allowed on our screens in Atlanta, because we consider it just a little bit too rugged for family audiences"—though, as Hefner pointed out, she apparently didn't find it too rugged for family TV screens.[8] It seems unbelievable that only ten years ago the Board of Censors in New York cut the scenes of the birth of a baby bison out of a Walt Disney wildlife feature, but continued to permit almost any representation of violent and sadistic death on the screen.[9] But best of all is the story of the head of the Memphis censor board who objected to a film because it contained a word she had never heard before: s-l-u-t.[10]

For myself, I applaud the *Playboy* protest against this kind of nonsensical hypocrisy, which, by pretending that sex is not there and by hiding the reality under Victorian euphemisms, makes it the more difficult to achieve any wholesome and positive understanding of the nature of sexuality. In addition, by concentrating its public wrath upon the supposed obscenity of sex, society all too easily detracts attention from the real evils of the day. I agree entirely with Howard Moody, who, in a recent article, wrote:

> For Christians the truly obscene ought not to be slick-paper nudity, nor the vulgarities of dirty old or young literati, nor even "weirdo" films showing transvestite orgies or male genitalia. What is obscene is that material, whether sexual or not, that has as its basic motivation and purpose the degradation, debasement and dehumanizing of persons. The dirtiest word in the English language is not "fuck" or "shit" in the mouth of a tragic shaman, but the word "NIGGER" from the sneering lips of a Bull Connor.[11]

Hefner himself admits that in the process of giving expression to the younger generation's revolt against sexual hypocrisy, some exaggeration and lack of proportion has resulted.

A freer, less taboo-ridden, less hypocritical society would probably have less interest in (and less need for) the rebel part of *Playboy*'s personality. . . . [Under the circumstances,] there is good reason to frequently emphasize and dramatize, overstate, burlesque and spoof, because we are expressing ourselves in a culture that has been so guilt-ridden and suppressed in these areas, that only such an aggressive approach stands a chance of counteracting the prevalent puritan set.[12]

The Attraction of the Illicit

Much of the excitement of nude photographs for the normal adolescent lies in the very fact that they are disapproved by society at large—and occasionally banned by authority. If we were honest enough to admit that we *all* enjoy a picture of a beautiful girl, there would be much less sniggering prurience and probably much less sexual deviation.[13] I suspect that much of the satisfaction that students get from plastering their walls with naked playmates comes from the fact that in this way they reaffirm their protest against their elders' view of sex as "dirty." Personally, my objection to many of the *Playboy* presentations of the female form is that they are too glossy and skin-deep, lacking in any human warmth—mere bodies and not people. There is more real, honest-to-goodness sexuality in many a nude by Bonnard or Modigliani than in a *Playboy* tease; but since the former have been open for view for fifty years or so, they apparently do not have the same status value. Once *Playboy* has made its point, perhaps it will offer us first-class reproductions of some of the great paintings of nudes in place of the frigid-looking models it sometimes dishes up at present.

Much of the humor in *Playboy* also seems to find its way into print only because it is supposedly illicit. Many of the jokes and cartoons would hardly be thought worth reproducing in a society which freely accepted its sexuality. They are, in fact, "dirty"—not because they are about sex, but because sex has been labeled dirty; and they are laughed at not because they are really clever or funny, but simply because they touch on a socially unacceptable subject. We have all experienced the situation in which someone announces that he has a story "for men only." Immediately, everyone present gets ready to roar with laughter—only to find that the story is often crude or banal, and would never be thought worth repeating except for its esoteric appeal. Most really subtle jokes or cartoons show up the vagaries or absurdities of human behavior or present a situation in which the subject speaks or acts in blatant contradiction to his actual circumstances. The oddities of our sexual inhibitions offer wonderful material for clever and entirely wholesome humor. Nothing but good can be done by helping people to laugh at their uncriticized stupidities without snickering embarrassment. Once again my criticism of *Playboy* is that it all too often proffers us the kind of joke which is only worth repeating because it presumes upon a rather childish community of interest in repudiating the traditional mores.

Once a healthy acceptance of sexuality has been achieved, the effect of this type of humor is minimal. Helmut Thielicke points out that there is a close parallel between nudity and sexual jokes. The truly naked human body, as in a Greek statue, arouses an aesthetic response of "disinterested delight," in Immanuel Kant's phrase, not libidinal excitement. Similarly, "the direct, unveiled telling of a downright dirty story would be quite as unsexual as the unveiled nudity of a statue—except that it would be unaesthetic. The story with a double meaning, however, provides the opportunity to 'undress' and in this symbolic analogy to act sexually, even though only in imagination." [14]

Is *Playboy* Antisexual?

It is true, of course, that our society has not yet achieved a healthy acceptance of sexuality. Probably we shall have to bear with the cruder type of *double-entendre* for a long time. Let us recognize that *Playboy,* despite its pandering to grade-school humor, serves a useful function in helping our society to free itself from prejudice and false taboos about sex.

But how far does *The Playboy Philosophy* go toward helping the student in the acquisition of a mature understanding of sex which will clear up his confusion and prevent a repetition of the same disasters in the next generation? At this point, Hefner has come under heavy fire from many who would grant that his crusade against prudery is entirely justified. But the nature of the criticism has been surprising. In an article which apparently helped to set in motion the unending editorials, and which has been included in his recent book *The Secular City,* Harvey Cox argues that *Playboy,* far from being too sexy, is antisexual.[15] "They dilute and dissipate authentic sexuality by reducing it to an accessory, by keeping it at a safe distance. . . . For *Playboy*'s man, others—especially women—are *for* him. They are his leisure accessories, his playthings." [16] Along a somewhat similar vein, *Time* magazine criticized the Playboy clubs as "brothels without a second story." [17]

To this type of objection, clever as it may be, I think Hefner has a valid answer. He can reply that there is a proper and justifiable place for sex as an aspect of entertainment and purely impersonal pleasure. Playboy clubs are hardly the only places in which people enjoy their meals more because they are served by pretty girls in reduced costumes—and many of these places are as respectable as the Bank of England. Does Cox propose to do away with chorus lines and ice shows because the girls employed in these occupations are not engaged in profound relationships with all the customers? Would the Playboy clubs be more acceptable if there *were* a second story? Provided that the girls so employed are treated as human beings and are not expected to go home with the customers after hours (which happens to be one of the strictest rules in this case), there seems to be little reason to single out Playboy clubs as antisexual. I tend to agree with Hefner that the need to express this kind of criticism may be rooted in the uneasiness that some critics feel with sex.[18]

The more penetrating criticism leveled by Cox and others is that *Playboy* inculcates a total philosophy of sex which fails to recognize the deeper levels of relationship involved and fails to offer any help in those relationships:

> Unlike the women he knows in real life, the *Playboy* reader's fictional girl friends know their place and ask for nothing more. They present no danger of permanent involvement. Like any good accessory, they are detachable and disposable . . . ; [but] much as the human male might like to terminate his relationship with a woman as he would snap off the stereo, or store her for special purposes like a camel's-hair jacket, it really can't be done. And anyone with a modicum of experience with women knows it can't be done. Perhaps this is the reason *Playboy*'s readership drops off so sharply after the age of thirty.[19]

The Point *Playboy* Misses

This is the real inadequacy of *Playboy*'s treatment of sex—not that it underplays sex or wrongly gives it a place in entertainment, but that it fails miserably to go beyond that and to recognize the complexities of sexuality once it moves from the glossy page or the Playboy Club and involves a real man and real woman in personal encounter. By consistently presenting sex as a commodity, as "one of the ingredients in [*Playboy*'s] total entertainment and service package for the young urban male," [20] the full psychological depths of sex are disguised. As Katherine Whitehorn wrote: "One thing that . . . the more joyous and confident revolutionaries leave out is that sex is *dangerous*. . . . It is a natural force, like fire; and like fire it can weld or warm or it can destroy." [21] By depicting sex as a simple, uncomplicated, easily controllable exercise in the enjoyment of the good life, *Playboy* misleads its readers into assuming that real women are as pliable, convenient, and usable as the playmate of the month—quite prepared to be folded up in three sections when the next attraction comes along. And the male reader is equally wrongly encouraged to suppose that he can approach sex in this manner without danger to his own integrity and maturity.

In fact, *The Playboy Philosophy* falls into precisely the same error as the traditional religious mores, which it castigates so vigorously: it denies the contemporary psychological understanding of the depths of sexuality in the human person. The churches have wrongly treated sex as a function of the body which can be readily disciplined or dispensed with without damage to the real self. *Playboy* treats it as a desirable accessory which can be changed according to the whim of the moment. Yet if we have learned anything from Freud and his successors, it is surely that we are not people with or without sex, as we choose, but sexual beings—and that to deny or degrade our sexuality is to degrade our very selves. "Sex," writes a contemporary British psychiatrist, "is so important, so pervasive, and so intimately connected with every aspect of personality, that it cannot be separated from the person as a whole without impoverishing even superficial relationships." [22]

The Yellow Rolls-Royce, a recent screenplay by Terence Rattigan, includes an effective object lesson in the complexities of sexual relations. The rich Lord Frinton, on the very day on which he fulfills a life-long ambition by winning the Gold Cup at Ascot, discovers his young French wife in the new Rolls in the arms of his assistant at the Foreign Office. The conversation of husband and wife on the way home in the car is a model of dramatic understatement in which the insoluble problems raised by this liaison are probed. Frinton, who adores his wife, assumes that she now finds him repugnant, and he cannot bear to think of her loving another man. She is, indeed, "mad about him, *voilà tout";* she assures her husband that she loves him, too, but admits that that is not enough. The third party, it is clear, had engaged in the relationship without any thought of its possible consequences and the pain it would cause, and was probably off with another girl by then. Rattigan very wisely does not attempt to unweave the web. Frinton remarks, somewhat overdramatically, "How I'm going to hate living after to-day," and sends the car back because "it displeases me." *Voilà tout,* in the movie; but we all know that in real life people have to go on living with all the pain of sex as well as its joys. Only on the screen, as in *The Yellow Rolls-Royce,* can the camera pass lightly on to the next amusing incident.

It is not so much what Hefner says, but what he leaves unsaid—and supplies by innuendo through cartoons and stories in the magazine—that disturbs me. On the surface his sentiments are unexceptionable:

> In my own moral view, I think there is a justifiable place for sex outside of wedlock. . . . It can . . . serve as a significant source of physical and emotional pleasure; it offers a means of intimate communication between individuals, and a way of establishing personal identification within a relationship and within society as a whole; it can become, at its best, a means of expressing the innermost, deepest felt longings, desires, and emotions.[23]

But what is meant by "sex" in this paragraph? Photographs of beautiful girls? A pretty "bunny" serving one's meals? A successful seduction? A profound love relationship between two responsible people? Promiscuous premarital intercourse? The total sexual involvement of a man and a woman in marriage? Are there, perhaps, sexual activities which destroy communication? Under what circumstances will sex establish personal identification? How is the young man to ensure that sex will express his (and the girl's) deepest longings and emotions rather than a purely superficial and selfish lust?

It is no reply to complain, as Hefner did in the first installment of *The Playboy Philosophy,* that such questions are unfair and irrelevant because the magazine makes no pretensions to cover the whole of human life and that such criticism is "like criticizing a good book of poetry because it includes no prose." The question is, rather, whether the two can be so easily distinguished, even in literature. Would a book that discussed only poetry in such a manner as to render the reader incapable of appreciating prose be a good book on poetry? Can the author of a work which has become the arbiter of taste and the guide of morals for millions of young Americans avoid the responsibility of discussing the deeper levels of sexual experience to which he so evangelistically wishes to introduce his readers?

The Inconsistency of *Playboy*

In fact, of course, Hefner has not maintained the distinction between entertainment sex and the problems it raises. The very existence of *The Playboy Philosophy,* and the difficulty of bringing it to any conclusion, witness to Hefner's recognition that there is no absolute distinction. He has said that he is "opposed to wholly selfish sex . . . , opposed to any human relationship that is entirely self-oriented—that takes all and gives nothing in return. . . . I do not believe that sexual behavior, or any other kind of behavior, should be irresponsible, and I'm strongly opposed to sexual exploitation, coercion, or aggression." [24] To say this is to recognize that sex contains potential elements of selfish exploitation, but it does little to clarify how such abuses are to be avoided. Nor does the average run of *Playboy* cartoons and stories suggest that the young man living life to the hilt with a full complement of cars, music, and playmates need give much attention to the danger. *Playboy* does not, indeed, provide its readers with a handy guide to "The Art of Seduction" in the straightforward manner of Albert Ellis in *Sex and the Single Man.*[25] But is it unfair to say that it leaves the reader with the impression that sexual intercourse is entirely desirable with any female body that can be persuaded to go to bed? Is there any suggestion that either the boy or the girl might want something more than this—or something less than this in the circumstances? Is there any recognition of the possibility that sexual relationships when carried to the logical conclusion may prove to have involved one of the partners far more deeply than the other? Is there any consideration of the implications of complete sexual freedom for the future of society or of marriage?

I put my objections in the form of questions because I personally find it very difficult to know what *The Playboy Philosophy* really intends to say to its devotees on these deeper matters —and even more difficult to know whether the general impact of the magazine corresponds to the editorial intention. Here, for example, is an important statement by Hefner:

It is wrong to suggest that we favor depersonalized sex. Not, unless, by depersonalized sex, we are referring to any and all sexual activity that does not include extensive involvement, commitments and obligations. . . . I certainly think that personal sex is preferable to impersonal sex, because it includes the greatest emotional rewards; but I can see no logical justification for opposing the latter unless it is irresponsible, exploitive, coercive, or in some way hurts one of the individuals involved.[26]

But what kind of sexual activity is appropriate without extensive involvement, commitments, and obligations? Do certain sexual intimacies *establish* some commitment to another human person? Does intercourse without obligations perhaps inevitably depersonalize the parties involved? How does one know when he is exploiting another individual? Can one exclude from one's consideration the possible hurt to her parents, future husband, or society at large?

I do not have, as will shortly become obvious, any pat answers to these questions. And my criticism of *Playboy* is not that it fails to answer them all, but that it fails to raise them— and by so doing gives the obvious impression that they can well be ignored. Taken for what it is—a good-natured spoofing of the stuffier aspects of our society, a much-needed protest against prudery and Comstockery, a forum for the discussion of sexual questions, a source of erotic relief for deprived males, a medium for occasional pieces of excellent writing, relaxing "Entertainment for Men"—*Playboy* fills a need. But that students should suppose that they are offered an adequate *philosophy* here, let alone a Bible, is disastrous.

Interestingly enough, recent studies have suggested that students are beginning to evolve their own philosophy of sex; but it is not that of *Playboy*. An early *Playboy* cartoon showed a crew-cut young man passionately embracing a girl in bed, and asking, "Why speak of love at a time like this?" More recently, the "Playboy Forum" has made it clear that although Hefner regards sexual activity with emotional involvement as preferable, he expressly rejects the view that there is a necessary or proper connection between sex and love.[27] Yet the indications are that today's students often find sexual intimacy without love meaningless and degrading, however momentarily pleasurable it may be. Gael Greene found that for women students, "cold fucking" —the blunt student phrase for the unfeeling act—is entirely unacceptable. "For the great majority of college girls," she writes, "sex without love is promiscuity, and promiscuity is undeniably a dirty word." [28] Perhaps the thinking of the more responsible male student is best expressed in the following statement, which the Kronhausens believed to be characteristic of a new sexual code emerging out of the present confusion:

"To sleep with a girl I do not love and who does not love me, even if she willingly agrees on a perfectly rational basis, is wrong, for these reasons:

(a) *Any casual sexual relationship goes against the feeling ingrained in me from childhood that sex and love are inextricably combined.* If I find they can be separated too easily and satisfactorily, it will take something away from my feelings about the relationship I will have with the girl I marry. It could also set up in me a habit pattern leading to later infidelity, a thing that would be destructive to my marriage relationship.

(b) It violates her personality. *Any girl's value to the man she wants to marry is cheapened more and more, the more boys she has slept with before him.*

[But, he continues,] *If we deeply love one another,* and we find in sex a way of showing its deepest levels; if we find that during and after and because of it we are both straining to grow in stature in the other's eyes; if we find that because it is loving, the release of the sex energy also releases, rather than uses up, our deepest creative energies; if each time there is a sexual interlude, we find we love and respect and admire each other more afterwards, then, and only then, but so sensitively and wonderfully then, *it is right*." [29]

This philosophy of sex is certainly not the traditional religious one. It carries implications which its advocates often fail to face up to. But it starts from a different assumption from that underlying *The Playboy Philosophy*, namely, that because sexual intercourse is properly and ideally the expression of personal love and commitment, its enjoyment without that relationship is not just a second best, but involves potential harm to the integrity and maturity of the persons concerned.

5

SEX, LUST, AND LOVE

"The Victorians, who talked a great deal about love, knew little about sex. Perhaps it is time that modern Americans, who know a great deal about sex, once again start talking about love." So *Time* magazine concluded its survey "The Second Sexual Revolution," thereby showing not only that its editors are capable of illuminating as well as reporting the state of "modern living," but also that *Time* is not quite so far ahead of us all as its publication a week in advance of the printed date line is intended to suggest.[1] For it seems clear, as we saw at the end of the last chapter, that student thinking has for some time been struggling to rediscover the relation between love and sex, and that a somewhat incoherent but definite connection between the two offers to young men and women a standard by which to judge or justify their sexual activities. As yet, however, the implications of such a criterion for morality have hardly been explored.

Some Definitions

I think we may clarify the issue if we attempt to define love and sex in relation to a third term, lust. The word "sex," as distinct from the fact, was invented by the Romans and first appears in literature in the writing of Cicero. Most philologists believe that it was derived from the word *secare,* to cut or sever, with an allusion to the Greek fable that human beings were originally bisexual until punished by Zeus with separation into male and female.[2] Well, *vive la différence;* but in the post-Freudian age, we no longer identify sex primarily with the anatomical distinctions between men and women. For us it is the raw psychophysical energy which affects all our relationships to other people from infancy on.[3] The tendency to use the terms "sex" and "sexual relations" as synonyms for coitus is entirely regrettable, although it occurs even in serious discussions of the subject. "Intercourse" has perhaps become so commonly identified with the full sex act that it cannot be rescued for wider usage. But sex and sexual relations begin long before intercourse is even physically possible, and include a wide range of acts or attitudes appropriate to many different personal contacts.

The re-emergence of sexual powers in the adolescent brings exciting new physical pleasure, entirely new ranges of relationship with boys or girls who were previously ignored or despised, and the discovery of emotional problems of which he was blissfully ignorant, but which few in later years would trade for the innocence of childhood. Sex, in its primal creative drive, transforms, enlivens, and expands his whole being. It excites his curiosity, colors all his thinking, stirs his imagination, and transforms his body. Sex moves him to dance and sing, to tease and explore, to caress and kiss. Some of his new sexuality involves the deepening or modification of existing relationships to parents, brothers, and sisters. Much of it is channeled through private "outlets" such as wet dreams or masturbation. For a long time, associations in groups, such as largely formal and impersonal public dates, provide all the sexual expression he needs. Despite (or perhaps because of) the disapproval of his elders, pictures or photographs or movies or books absorb his sexual interest. But sooner or later, for most adolescents, sexuality becomes focused on one particular person; and here he is faced with the possibility of lust or love—or, more probably, of some combination of the two.

Lust is by no means exclusively a sexual attitude, but for our present purpose we may define it as the desire for or use of another human being conceived as the object of purely selfish pleasure. Lust is concerned with the fulfillment of its own desire without thought of the interests of the other person. Lust isolates the physical aspect of sex and asks no questions about its deeper implications. Lust tries to satisfy its own unhappiness or insecurity or greed by snatching at any available source. Lust gratifies itself without concern for the hunger of its partner —or its plaything. Lust is sex gone sour. James Gould Cozzens's best-selling novel should surely have been entitled *By Lust Possessed.* Lust may use the language of love—lust may persuade itself that it loves; but it lacks even the insight of self-love, let alone the capacity to love another. As an English writer has recently put it:

He who is able to love himself is able to love others also, for he has understood his true value and does not need to bolster up his own value by snatching it from others. When I am unaware of what I truly am, I am incapable of giving myself value, and so I desperately seek value from someone else; and this leads me to action which is sometimes identified with sex; but with sex divorced from its true object, which is the completion of the union of two people who have found their own value, and therefore found value in each other. So the inadequate heterosexual goes in search of the prostitute, the inadequate homosexual in search of the "queer" bar—because neither knows value in themselves or in another.[4]

There are, mercifully, few human beings in whom lust exclusively directs their sexual powers. When they come to light in the courts, we recognize such unfortunates as psychopaths. When the Don Juan ends up on the psychiatrist's couch, he is recognized as a sick man, haunted by fears about his own masculinity and incapable of mature sexual relationships. But there are those who advocate something very close to pure lust, like Albert Ellis, in his chapter "The Art of Seduction" in *Sex and the Single Man:*

Even girls who *don't* want to be talked into having sex relations with a male can frequently be persuaded [he assures us], for most girls have exceptionally poor reasons for not indulging, and these reasons can often be logically undermined. . . . One of the best persuasive methods for getting a girl to go further than she originally intends is

> to convince her that you are not necessarily asking that she have actual intercourse with you, but you are largely trying to induce her to have some form of mutually satisfying relations that will result in orgasm for both of you. . . . On the whole, even from the very first night you make any passes at your girl friend—which may well be the first time you meet her—you should try to go as far as you can possibly go with her sexually: since, much to your surprise, you may even be able to go all the way right at the start; and usually the further you get with her this time, the further you are likely to get with her the next time.[5]

If the girl is unresponsive to immediate intimacy and cannot be conned into bed, Ellis advises the single man to peddle his attentions elsewhere.[6] Romantic attachments have their place, but they tend to lead to marriage, which, though always reversible, is often inhibiting.[7] In any case, love is not necessary for full sex enjoyment: "Sex that is engaged in without love (or even friendship) can certainly be, and in innumerable cases is, one of the most satisfying of human pursuits." [8]

Sexual love does, of course, include an element of desire and possession. The satisfaction of petting or intercourse is no less physically enjoyable within the relationship of love. Only a Tristan would have thought of denying the physical aspect of romantic devotion by placing his sword, at the moment of passion, between Isolde and himself.[9]

The difference between lust and love is not that one is sexy and the other ethereal. In the relationship of love, another person is encountered as a self, not as a thing. The girl is enjoyed not purely for what the boy gets out of it, but for what she is in herself—not only as a body but as a person. He is concerned not only with his own satisfaction but with hers—and with all her hesitancies, fears, needs, and aspirations. "Being in love is the most selfless of experiences; we are taken out of ourselves and concerned only with the other; the self that desires drops out of the picture. That is why lovers as such are humble. There is no squinting round to see oneself as desiring—it is an almost outward-looking condition." [10] The Russian writer Vladimir Solovyov, in a frequently quoted book, *The Meaning of Love,* put the point more philosophically:

The meaning and value of love as a feeling consists in the fact that it makes us actually, with our whole being, recognize in *another* the absolute central significance which owing to egoism we feel in ourselves only. Love is important, not as one of our feelings, but as the transference of our whole vital interest from ourselves to another, as the transposition of the very center of our personal life.[11]

Sex, in this case, is not something to be used for itself, but an expression of and a fulfillment of the most profound human relationship possible. This, I take it, is the essence of the position stated by the student at the conclusion of the previous chapter—that sleeping with a girl whom one does not love, using her merely as a means of self-gratification, seeing sex as a pleasure to be got out of her, rather than as a means of personal union with her, is the really immoral thing—the denial of something essentially right and good.

The Philosophy of Self-Interest

I shall have more to say in later chapters about how this principle of love applies. For the moment I want to suggest that if I am right in the contrast I have drawn between lust and love, we have uncovered a quite fundamental contradiction between the philosophy of many honest students and that of self-interest. For if love means anything at all, it means that in the most crucial and intimate issues of a man's life, his concern is not for himself but for another. And this is exactly what Ellis and those who share his view will not, or cannot, acknowledge. The real roots and the full consequences of his sexual ethics come out in the following very honest but, to most responsible people, appalling statement of egotistical hedonism:

You have to keep in mind, pretty constantly, that your main goal in life, in the seventy-five or so years that you have to exist on this earth, is enjoyment. Yes, peculiarly enough: *enjoyment*. . . . You are not here primarily to achieve something wonderful during your life-time, to be of great service to others, to change the course of the world, or to do anything else but (in one way or another that you find particularly appealing) to enjoy yourself.[12]

Ellis does admit that self-interest will from time to time involve some respect for the good of others. Minors and mental defectives should be avoided because they cannot give free consent to the seducer. We should refrain from needlessly and deliberately harming another human being; but, ultimately, concessions to the interests of others should be temporary and quite secondary:[13] "Your main goal should still be to find what is most pleasing, most satisfying to *you;* and then doing [*sic*] those things, if they are feasible, no matter what others may tend to think of you for doing them. Naturally, you must be somewhat sensible about how others take to your goals and aims, and must not unduly antagonize them—*especially when they have some power over you.*" [14]

Of course, there are times when all of us fall into the mood of despair which sees life as nothing more than a grasping after private pleasure. There are periods when the national mood of a great nation takes on this color. In the nineteen-fifties it was generally characteristic of American student aspirations. But a generation which is deeply concerned about underdeveloped countries and the struggle for racial equality reflects a philosophy founded on respect for people as people, and a concern to live for more than individual satisfaction. Nor do young men who give their time and energy—and even risk their lives—in such causes do so merely because they fear that the spread of communism or the ultimate triumph of Negro rights may otherwise inconvenience their own futures. They are not merely concerned with the opinions and needs of those who have power over them. Equally, I believe that the student who is caught up in the joy and pain of love for another person finds the philosophy of "enlightened self-interest" entirely inadequate. His relationship with his girl lifts him out of the nicely calculated rationalism which subordinates sexuality to private pleasure. He is grasped by a love which reorientates his life round another and round her interests. He finds himself doing what is more pleasing and satisfying not for himself but for this other being. There is agony as well as ecstasy in mature sexual relationship; but there is also the realization that sex finds its meaning and fullness in the expression of self-giving and mutual growth. The Ellis prescription is then seen in all its superficiality.

The Religious Dimension of Love

In an earlier chapter, I argued that religion, as it has come to be practiced or rejected in our world, is largely irrelevant to the student's understanding of his sexuality. But now I want to suggest that sex may not be irrelevant to religion; rather, when sex is subsumed in and irradiated by love rather than by lust, by self-giving rather than by self-seeking, it confronts us with a mystery beyond our analysis and calls forth a response of respect and awe which is essentially religious. It is no mere chance that one of the favorite expressions of the young man in love is, "I adore you," and that the seventeenth-century marriage service of the Anglican Church (still used in England) required the bridegroom to pledge to the bride, "With my body I thee worship."

Colin MacInnes, whom nobody who knows his writing will suspect of ecclesiastical conformity, in the article quoted earlier, "Coming of Age in Great Britain," [15] described the "liberal-permissives" in these terms:

> These are persons whose sexual attitudes are largely determined by a defiant rejection of the Christian ethos: if the Church says sex is solemn, and its abuses sin, they say both are neither. This gives to their sexual judgments and behavior a marked degree of tolerance—or perhaps indifference—but deprives these of much weight and

beauty. For after all, there *is* a religious element in sexual union: it is the only miracle most of us will ever know: a recreation of ourselves through someone else, and thus a sacrament.

A recent collection of informal conversations with young men and women, also from England, contained one account of falling in love which had the quality of religious conversion. An eighteen-year-old man, who described himself as an "ex-tough" with good reason, gave this description of the relationship which had changed his life:

It's funny about Carol. She's different from all the other girls I've known. I feel as if I really belong with her, you know. She's everything I've always wanted. . . . She's got principles. She wouldn't sleep with me until we're married. She's everything—good looking, a good family and the same interests as me. I really fell in love with her after we'd known each other for about three months. We really began to be close to each other then; not intimate, but close. There's a magnetism between us. If I lost her I'd sort of die, I'd go mad. I'm sometimes afraid that she might go off with someone else, but I don't think she would. If I search for years, a million years, I'd never find anyone like her. She's all I live for, all I work for. I see her as much as I can, but not every night. I can't go wrong with her.[16]

Here is a man whose life had been self-centered, promiscuous, irresponsible, but who, in love, finds himself in second place to another who is "all I live for."

It is true, of course, that romantic sexual love embodies various degrees of lust which may become predominant. It is true that exclusive love for one girl can be an obsession, which, instead of opening up the possibilities of love towards family or neighbor, builds barriers of possessiveness and jealousy.[17] It is true that the sentimental "love on a pink cloud . . . happily ever after" theme of much third-rate literature and most of our popular songs is in itself inadequate as a basis for marriage. Ernest Havemann is quite right when he says, "Love, the magic spell is everywhere—like a choking smog settling over the land, corroding the lungs of the Jane Does and John Smiths of America, poisoning them against the bracing delights of reality." [18]

Unless it is balanced by an honest assessment of the real strengths and weaknesses of the lover, and given backbone by serious and rational intention, romantic love will soon evaporate under the strains of marriage. Emotional imagination must be complemented by a readiness to accept faults and disillusion, to make sacrifices and submit to discipline. But my argument is that romantic love, at least as it is experienced by many students, does have at least the germ of this quality within it. I am arguing that the experience of sex is often the channel through which a young man becomes aware, however dimly, of a reality which is ultimate, beyond the neat definition of scientific observation, inconsistent with the ethics of self-interest, and capable of transforming and overwhelming the self-centeredness of the individual.

Some writers on this theme attempt to denigrate romantic love on the ground that it is non-Christian in origin, and relatively new. But the fact that this ideal originated outside the official religious tradition is hardly a sound reason for rejecting it today—the same is true of our modern belief in the value of the individual, political and religious toleration, and the scientific method. Moreover, it can be argued that this concept of personal relations is implicit in the biblical view of God and man, and that its reaffirmation outside the church was inspired (however unconsciously) by a better grasp of Christian origins than the contemporary ecclesiastical world knew. It seems to me that those religious thinkers who, like C. S. Lewis, disparage romantic love and envision its decline with equanimity are cutting themselves off from a vital means of communication with the younger generation of today and tomorrow. Of course, if you define religion in terms of a system of thought or a code of ethics, today's students, with their repudiation of authority and their sexual enthusiasm, will appear beyond hope. But if we follow a widespread trend in contemporary theology and think of religion as concerned with the boundary of man's existence or the depths of his being, then the relevance of sex to religion will be apparent.[19] Harvey Cox, in the book already referred to, has argued that secular man does experience the transcendent, even though he does not call it by the traditional name of God. Theology is not concerned to defend the letters G-O-D, but to interpret the experience of man as he confronts that which he cannot possess or master but which comes to him. The transcendent, he writes, is "that which is not part of the self's equipment, but comes from beyond the self. No doubt urban-secular man experiences the transcendent in a radically different *way* than did his tribal and town forebears. He may find it, as Bonhoeffer once said, 'in the nearest Thou at hand,' but he does meet it. It is his experience of the transcendent which makes man man." [20]

I suggest that for many students sexual love has and always will have this quality of religious awareness within it. Our human love is often ephemeral and unrealistic, frequently distorted by lust, always to some degree self-centered; but insofar as it is true to its highest character, it is not concerned with self-interest, however enlightened, but with self-giving. The man who knows what it is to serve and care for, to honor and desire, a girl for no other reason than that she is who and what she is has some understanding of true religion. Martin Buber has taught us that it is a denial of the biblical concept of creation to look for God *outside* our everyday experience of people. It is not after, or in addition to, or as a consequence of, our meeting the Thou of another person that we meet the eternal Thou—it is *in* the Thou that God is known.[21] Dietrich Bonhoeffer wrote in his *Letters from Prison*: "Speaking frankly, to long for the transcendent when you are in your wife's arms is, to put it mildly, a lack of taste, and it is certainly not what God expects of us. We ought to find God and love him in the blessings he sends us. If he pleases to grant us some overwhelming earthly bliss, we ought not to try and be more religious than God." [22]

Man's Love and God's Love

Christians are convinced that there is a standard of self-giving love to which we ought to conform our personal relations, and by which the adequacy of our sex lives can be judged. And they find the historical embodiment of such a standard in the person of Jesus Christ. This is the essence of the traditional theological doctrine of the deity of Jesus—the conviction that his life and death exhibited a quality of human self-giving, a capacity to be "the man for others" rather than for himself, which cannot be explained from within the human sphere. Jesus did not convince his early followers by laying claim to traditional evidences of religious authority. The only reason a few people took him seriously was that they were fascinated by the inexplicable and compelling appearance in their midst of one man in whom they saw the perfection of the love which they so inadequately practiced. And the only way they could express this bizarre conviction was by describing him as "Son of God"—the temporal reflection of eternal love.

I think that a valid distinction can be drawn between *Christ* and the religion which bears his name. The latter is indeed at present—though not necessarily forever—irrelevant to the great majority of students. The former, I would maintain, offers the only adequate basis for a mature and coherent view of sex—a view which the man who recognizes love as a decisive criterion already partly shares.

The reader of any literature dealing with the history of sexual customs or the relation of religion and sex will notice that even the most extreme critics of the Christian tradition are usually careful to exempt Jesus from their strictures. St. Paul is commonly, though not always justly, pictured as the villain responsible for introducing Hellenistic dualism into an otherwise healthy sexual tradition in early Christianity. For example, Hugh Hefner writes: "The Christian view of sex and the female as inherently sinful did not come from Christ. It was derived largely from the teachings of St. Paul, who was influenced by the asceticism of the Asiatic religions then spreading throughout the Roman Empire." [23] Now, this readiness to exempt Jesus from the general castigation of religion reflects some grasp of the fact that Jesus was not antisexual. He did not single out sensual sins for special condemnation. The list of evils about which Jesus warned his disciples included only two specifically sexual sins, adultery and fornication, out of thirteen—and he emphasized that the source of distortion was in the heart of man, not in his body.[24] There is absolutely no indication that Jesus, like some of his later followers, regarded women as agents of the devil. The comment of one of the more liberal of the church fathers, Clement of Alexandria, to the effect that "every woman should blush at the thought that she is a woman," is entirely inconceivable on the lips of Jesus. He mixed and ate with prostitutes, and one of them became his close follower. Lewinsohn remarks: "In no other religion does a female sexual-sinner figure in so important a role. The figure of Mary Magdalene typifies tolerance carried to the highest degree." [25] When Jesus taught that looking at a woman "to lust after her" [26] involves adultery in the heart, there is no reason to suppose that he was condemning all and every male enjoyment of the beauty of a woman's body outside of marriage. Lust, as we have seen, implies the purely selfish desire to possess another person. And in any case the commandment is not quoted in order to emphasize the singular seriousness of sexual sin, but as an illustration of the fact that evil cannot be measured by outward acts alone. Indeed, this saying is a repudiation of precisely the kind of legalism in sexual matters of which the churches have been most guilty.

The early church soon began to devote itself to the production of detailed codes governing the lives of its members. But, as C. H. Dodd has pointed out, they differ from the teaching of Jesus in being directly applicable to the day-to-day life of a

Christian living in a pagan world. They include instructions about family responsibilities, relations with non-Christians in work and social life, duties toward the government, and, of course, specific rules for sexual conduct.[27] In contrast, the Sermon on the Mount sets forth an absolute standard of love with which every man has to come to terms, but which cannot be reduced to a tidy set of rules. Bishop John Robinson writes:

> Regarded as a code of conduct, prescribing what one should do in any situation, the Sermon on the Mount is quite impracticable. It tears the individual loose from any horizontal nexus. In any given precept it rules out of consideration all other interests, all other values, all other people. . . . It is entirely inadequate [judged as a code]. It says nothing whatever, for instance, about how a man is to pursue what after all occupies most of our waking hours (when we are not being slapped in the face or asked for our coat), namely our everyday work, or how one is to be a good citizen and a positive and useful member of society.[28]

In fact, Jesus refused to follow the rabbinic tradition of developing a precise system of religious regulations. The chief cause of his struggle with the authorities of Judaism lay in his claim that the love of God and man is supreme over all law. He cut through the smoke screen that obscured the primacy of love and demanded that each man should work out his own responsibility in its light, rather than seek a false security in the observance of other people's wishes or commands. Paul Tillich has stated the effect very well:

> The burden He wants to take from us is the burden of religion. It is the yoke of the law, imposed on the people of His time by the religious leaders, the wise and the understanding, as He calls them in their own words—the Scribes and Pharisees, as they are called usually. Those who labor and are heavy laden are those who are sighing under the yoke of the religious law. And he will give them the power to overcome religion and law; the yoke He gives them is a "new being" above religion.[29]

Jesus and Sexuality

Jesus' refusal to take up the position of a judge on sexual issues is illustrated by a story which has been a perpetual stumbling block to the more rigoristic of his disciples. His critics brought before him a woman taken in the very act of adultery, a clear-cut case of breaking the law which was punishable by death. Jesus refused at first to give an opinion, but when pressed replied to her accusers, "That one of you who is faultless shall throw the first stone," and to the woman, when all had withdrawn in disarray, "No more do I [condemn you]. You may go; do not sin again." [30]

Some have thought that the silence of Jesus at the beginning of this story, and the enigmatic reference to his bending down and writing on the ground with his finger, arose from his embarrassment at being confronted with so indelicate a situation. But this only reflects the traditional difficulty that Christians have had in accepting the fact that Jesus lived a human life which included close association with the riffraff of society. Popular portraits frequently show him as an effeminate, sexless nonentity, and Swinburne's "pale Galilean" myth still colors our reading of the Gospels. But orthodoxy has always maintained, in theory at least, that Jesus was fully man, and manhood without sexuality is unimaginable. He seems to have accepted his manhood without anxiety and without exaggeration. He certainly did not share our obsession with sex; but neither is there anywhere in the New Testament portrait any suggestion of the antisexualism of Hellenistic Christianity. Tom F. Driver, in an article to which I am greatly indebted, concludes:

> Over against the pagan gods and the pagan religions we may say that Jesus appears as the great neutralizer of the religious meaning of sex. He does not, it is clear, regard sexuality as a mystical force emanating from the God-head. Jesus is no Dionysius. But contrary to what many Christians have assumed, the Jesus of the Gospels is not plainly "anti-Dionysian" either. That is, he does not as far as

we can tell regard sexuality as a force emanating from Satan. This opinion was left to the Gnostics to develop, who found some remarks of St. Paul to encourage them, and who have had a profound influence on the history of Christianity. Our modern ambivalence about sex, according to which it is either the best or the worst of all things, is Gnostic in origin and Manichaean in character.[31]

The remark of the psychiatrist Anthony Storr is relevant to the understanding of Jesus' personality:

> We are not, and cannot be, disembodied; and so our attitude to our own bodies and to those of other people is an important part of our total feeling towards even those with whom we may never exchange any more intimate gesture than a handshake. It is because of this that those who are ill-at-ease with their own sexuality are often detached and remote; for they are unable to allow their sexual selves to be manifest, and thus withdraw, both physically and psychologically, from the possibility of close contact. On the other hand, those who have been able to find sexual happiness are not generally afraid of intimacy, and are thus less guarded and more able to interchange experiences at even purely social levels of relationship.[32]

The totally natural manner of Jesus' relationships with men and women suggests that he achieved a harmony of the self and of sexuality which set him free to fulfill his special vocation as the servant of God. Few, I think, will suggest that Jesus showed signs of emotional or psychic disorder. His understanding of his mission made marriage impossible for him in practice—though why it should be assumed that it was in principle excluded escapes me, since he did enjoy a unique and intimate relationship with one particular woman, his mother Mary. Whether the temptations which he experienced included the choice between marriage and the fulfillment of his calling as Son of Man, as Nikos Kazantzakis suggested in his speculative novel *The Last Temptation of Christ,* we cannot know. But the lack of any such suggestion in the Gospels may reflect only the embarrassment of later Christians over the whole matter, and it seems difficult for those who maintain that he was "tested every way, only without sin" to deny the possibility.[33] What does seem certain, if we are to recognize in Jesus one who lived a human life and affected the human sphere, is that his love for his friends was not asexual. Our knowledge of the role of sex in childhood and adolescence, as well as the realization that all man-woman relationships have a sexual element, makes such a position absurd. This does not, of course, give any license to the prurient to uncover illicit liaisons between Jesus and Mary Magdalene. Contemporary Jewish standards of sexual behavior were strict, and politicians then as now would have been quick to undermine the authority of a rival religious teacher if they could have dug up even the suspicion of deviate behavior. However difficult it may be for the pious or the libertine to swallow, Jesus seems to have lived a life of complete sexual normality, neither fleeing the body in distaste, nor suffering any psychic trauma because he was possessed by a passion strange to our self-centered ways—though not altogether unknown to the man who is taken out of himself by love.

6 DOING WHAT COMES NATURALLY

The assumption that there are certain practices or attitudes which constitute the natural or normal pattern of human behavior has a long and checkered history. Today it is represented by the well-nigh universal student opinion that the healthy young man will do himself some physical or psychic damage if he refrains from giving free expression to his sexual instincts. Both those who do and those who do not tend to take it for granted that to abstain from intercourse after adolescence is symptomatic of some inadequacy. The popular misconceptions about what Freud had to say about repression and the ugly consequences of ignoring one's sexual drives seem to leave students with the alternatives of serious neurosis or immediate sexual gratification. The scorn heaped upon the idea of "sublimation" has the effect of undermining the morale of many who might otherwise exercise some restraint. The acceptance of Kinsey's figures as the norm of sexual activity puts a considerable portion of the male population under obligation to doubt their virility or to engage in sexual adventures which hold little attraction for them.

Sex as Unnatural

To say of a certain practice that it is "natural" is to invest it with a certain authority, to suggest its inevitability or its appropriateness, to imply that in disregarding it we deny our humanity. What is natural is, by suggestion, elevated above the local and parochial and endowed with ultimate significance or at least with universal status. It is understandable, therefore, that societies of all kinds, religious and secular, find it convenient to bolster their particular insights by labeling them as "natural" and proper to mankind—the implication being not only that they are now seen to be desirable and good, but that they are inherent to the human race and have only been ignored out of malice or perversity. Religious thinking about sex has participated to the full in this unconscious deception. I am not here prejudging the question whether there is in fact a concept of human behavior which is closer than any other to a divinely intended pattern, nor the question whether there are certain moral prohibitions (e.g., against murder) which are universally recognized. I am pointing out that much of what moralists and lawyers have sonorously pronounced "natural" in the sphere of sexual ethics is now known to be nothing of the sort.

Homosexual acts have been condemned with peculiar vehemence as "unnatural" because it was quite wrongly supposed that they were unknown in the animal world; in fact, this particular sexual phenomenon is prevalent in the subhuman sphere and is especially common among the primates.[1] Indeed, the Marquis de Sade argued that sodomy was good because it is an impulse found in nature. Many State statutes contain laws against "the abominable and detestable crime against nature," a phrase used to include all manner of sexual activities to which Victorian society objected, many of which are not only taken for granted in most primitive societies, but have also been accepted in some advanced civilizations.[2] We now know that many prohibitions which the church has hardly felt it necessary to defend, because they were supposedly so obviously and unquestionably right in the eyes of all men, run counter to the mores of some great culture of the past. Abortion was legally and socially acceptable among the Romans, homosexual love was practiced by the Greeks and praised by Plato, the Ptolemies of Egypt married their own brothers and sisters without apparent ill effects for 300 years. Prostitution is one of the earliest human institutions, and it has been more often than not officially organized and frequently given religious sanction. Indeed, within the Christian Era there has taken place a striking revision of attitude toward prostitution. Both St. Augustine and St. Thomas Aquinas accepted the institution as a necessary safety valve for the protection of "honest matrons." [3] The revolution in our thinking on this subject has come about not through the insights of the church, but as a result of the new appreciation of the worth of women which originated in the ideal of romantic love.[4]

One of the last bastions of the "natural law" principle in sexual morality has been the distinction—now apparently about to be abandoned—between natural and unnatural methods of contraception. Originally, as we have noted, theologians allowed that pleasure in coitus within marriage was not blameworthy provided that the act was engaged in with the goal of, or at least the chance of, procreation. In practice, Catholic moralists have quietly modified the principle to admit the justification of intercourse during the "safe period." [5] One argument in favor of linking sexual enjoyment with conception, which was widely used in the Middle Ages and is even repeated by Catholic and Protestant writers today, is the belief that by divine ordination the female desire for sexual experience coincides with ovulation.[6] The inference is that since it is natural for her to enjoy intercourse when she is most likely to conceive, the satisfaction of her sexual desire at other times is unnecessary or perverse. The difficulty, of course, is that the facts are entirely against the theory. In the great majority of women, sexual desire is at its height just before the menstrual cycle when conception is least likely.[7] If we are going to employ nature as a norm for sexuality, it appears that the mutual enjoyment of intercourse without procreation is at least as divinely planned as its enjoyment when conception is possible. Indeed, the evidence (insofar as it is relevant at all) points in the opposite direction. Since it is characteristic of the higher animals, including man, to desire sexual play at times when the female is not in oestrus, whereas in the lower animals the two coincide, it can be argued that "*having* sexual relations for reproduction alone is bestial, not vice-versa." [8]

The inadequacies of the traditional definition of what is natural in sex do not arise only from the fallacy involved in claiming universal validity for particular ethical ideals. These might be entirely desirable in themselves if they were distinguished from the insecure foundation on which they have been erected. But the orthodox position involves the further absurdity of saying, in effect, "doing what comes naturally is usually unnatural." The fundamental contradiction is epitomized in the traditional attitude toward masturbation, which we shall consider in the next chapter. The sense of guilt established in our culture by two thousand years and more of horrified condemnation of a practice which is an almost universally necessary phase of sexual development distorts the whole moral system of the church.

The roots of this guilt are to be found in the dualistic concept of man which so quickly came to dominate Christian thought after the death of Jesus. We have seen that he was able to accept his sexuality and that of others without embarrassment or anxiety. He certainly was not unaware of the possibilities of abuse and depravity in sexual relations—how could he have been when he numbered prostitutes among his friends? But his attitude toward the joys and opportunities of human life was essentially positive and open. Larger demands and wider love inevitably restricted his own development of sexual relationships, yet he never gave any credence to the idea that this sphere of human enjoyment was to be treated as unclean or base. Yet this is exactly what his followers have done because, unlike Jesus, they have adopted a view of man which contrasts flesh and spirit, natural and supernatural, the actual self and the ideal self. St. Paul can, I think, be defended against the accusation that he is responsible for this dualism. But it was certainly not difficult for subsequent thinkers to interpret his writing as if he condemned all sexual pleasure as evil.[9]

The consequence is that Christians from infancy are imbued with a point of view which is entirely inconsistent with the development of a mature sex life.[10] The fact that it is acknowledged that most of them will not attain the ideal (i.e., complete abstinence from sexual activity or its restriction to marriage) does not greatly reduce the sense of unconscious fear and failure. The achievement of a balanced selfhood is made much more difficult by an inbuilt sense of incompetence and depravity. H. A. Williams, in his contribution to *Objections to Christian Belief*, pointed out that the message of the churches amounts to, "Stop doing a, b, c. Tell God you are sorry for doing them and start trying to do x, y, and z"—a message that is psychologically disastrous. The result is as follows:

> The possibility of vision is excluded from the start. The path of increasing awareness is blocked. And if something within me tells me this is so, if a voice within hints that I am being disloyal to what I truly am—well, such things are never felt explicitly or articulated in any clear message. I merely feel that being a Christian is being a strain, and for that complaint the clergyman has an answer ready to hand. Jesus told us it would be difficult to follow Him. It is such an easy, plausible and seductive lie. . . . For life and behavior based on feelings of guilt excludes charity. To be bullied, compelled, by subtle inner unidentifiable fear to apparent worship and goodness is to destroy the self.[11]

To accept as the law of his nature a set of negative prohibitions, the effect of which is to question precisely what he feels to be the core of his humanity, involves for the student a denial of integrity which he cannot and should not accept. If the Christian churches are to speak to him, they have to discover, or recover, a concept of wholeness in sex which is derived from a deeper understanding of man as he actually is. Instead of starting from the assumption and exaggeration of a conflict within the self, we must understand man as a being who has to grow in relationship to others. In the words of Canon Douglas Rhymes: "Man is not a dualism of the lower and the higher. Man is a whole being set in relationship to a whole being, subject not to conflict between two laws but to relationship with the ground of his being who is God mirrored in Christ, and to responsible relationships . . . with other beings with whom he realizes the love which is the root of his existence." [12]

The Tyranny of Statistics

It is not surprising that there has been a vigorous reaction against the religious legalism which, in the name of "nature," denies the goodness of sex and the integrity of the person. But the popular alternative—the indiscriminate affirmation of the goodness of sex—may well involve us in a new bondage to the tyranny of statistics. The fact that a majority of the members of our society engage in a particular activity which is repudiated by the official code is a very good reason for examining both the activity and the code; but it is not a very good reason for abandoning the code wholesale without discrimination or intelligent discussion. Almost every driver of an automobile in the country breaks the speed limit from time to time; but this fact is not in itself a sound reason to eliminate all speed limits. Heart disease, probably a partial product of our affluent but anxious social order, is on the increase; but we do not for that reason take it for granted that nothing should be done to reduce it. I am not suggesting that there is a direct parallel between any of these facts and the revolution in sexual patterns over the past fifty years. I merely want to raise some pertinent questions about the use of figures such as those of the Kinsey reports as a justification for the immediate gratification of every sexual urge. Can we argue that *because* more than 60 per cent of all college-level males pet to orgasm, it is a desirable and satisfactory practice? Is it necessarily true that because Kinsey found that the great majority of the male population have premarital intercourse, the trend is ever upward and onward and that the few who hold out are mere relics of an evolutionary stage which the human race has left behind? Do statistics provide us with a criterion of what is "natural"—and if so, what is it?

It must be emphasized that Kinsey did make a valiant effort to discourage the use of his material as if it prejudged the moral and ethical issues. He carefully used the contrast "frequent/rare" rather than "normal/abnormal" with its subjective and emotive associations.[13] He repeatedly emphasized that his researches had *not* discovered or established a single uniform "American sexual pattern":

> There is no American pattern of sexual behavior, but scores of patterns, each of which is confined to a particular segment of our society. Within each segment there are attitudes on sex and patterns of overt activity which are followed by a high proportion of the individuals in that group; and an understanding of the sexual mores of the American people as a whole is possible only through an understanding of the sexual patterns of all of the constituent groups.[14]

Kinsey was very careful to make it clear that statistical information cannot determine the value of the practices it records. After a full statement of the arguments *pro* and *con* premarital coitus, he concluded with this warning—which has gone almost entirely unheeded:

> The resolution of these conflicting claims can come only through some recognition that certain of these problems lie in areas which belong to the biologic, psychologic, and social sciences, while others are moral problems which the student of moral philosophies must solve. Even the scientific aspects are too many for any immediate solution; but the data brought together in the present chapter may contribute to a more objective understanding of certain aspects of the problem.[15]

Without doubt the work of Kinsey and his associates has contributed enormously to the task of reaching intelligible and responsible judgments about sexual activity. It has been said, with some reason, that his initial reports will rank with Karl Marx's *Das Kapital,* Darwin's *Origin of Species,* and Adam Smith's *The Wealth of Nations* in their influence on history.[16] But unfortunately the influence of the reports is largely vitiated by the widespread disregard of the author's warnings of the limitations inherent in this kind of study.

Limitations of the Kinsey Reports

In the first place, references to Kinsey seldom bother to make any distinction between the different kinds of "outlets" referred to in the study. For example, Kinsey provides a chart showing the average sexual outlets between adolescence and age thirty, from which it appears that the majority of the men interviewed had between one and four orgasms regularly each week.[17] Kinsey chose the very clinical (though oddly masculine) term "outlet" to avoid any judgment as to the adequacy or desirability of particular experiences. The statistical basis for the chart included, indiscriminately, orgasm resulting from wet dreams, masturbation, petting, intercourse within and outside marriage, contacts with animals, and homosexual associations. As a basis for assessing the total animal sexuality of the male population, the figures are useful enough; but as a basis for establishing a norm of meaningful or truly personal sexual experience, they are worthless. Whether most of these achievements of physical orgasm were at all expressive of love, or whether they were in any way capable of carrying that weight, we do not know.

Ashley Montagu, in an early criticism of the first Kinsey report, pointed out the dangers inherent in the indiscriminate use of large figures:

> The authors are careful not to give the accolade of their sanction to any of the forms of behavior they describe. But since, in America, *quantity* is a moral value which makes acceptable and normalizes what in lesser quantities would be unacceptable and abnormal, the conclusion most likely to be drawn is that what has hitherto been thought unacceptable and abnormal must now be accepted and regarded as normal.[18]

He goes on to argue that the mere fact that more than six million adult Americans have homosexual tendencies is no more reason for accepting that condition as natural than the fact that millions of us have criminal tendencies justifies abolishing the courts. There are, indeed, materials for some kind of discrimination built into the Kinsey reports, though they are all too frequently ignored. For his figures showed that advancing education resulted in marked differences in sexual activity. A generation before, Lewis Terman had anticipated that within a few decades premarital intercourse would be universal. Kinsey found that Terman's expectations were based on inadequate samples and faulty procedures.[19] In fact, he concluded that the trend in the general population was not toward more premarital intercourse, but away from it as the percentage of young people going on to college increased.[20] Equally striking was the difference between the lower and the higher educational groups in their attitude to and use of prostitutes. Nearly three out of four in the grade-school class visited a prostitute before they were twenty-five; but among college graduates the percentage was hardly more than one in four.[21] Kinsey reported that students found this experience almost always unsatisfactory;[22] and the Kronhausens noted that in some cases the impersonal nature of experience with a prostitute had soured a student's sex life permanently.[23]

The significance of these variations cannot be assessed without recognizing that alternative practices, such as petting to orgasm, have largely taken the place of intercourse with dates or prostitutes in the college-level group. The validity of these alternatives we shall consider later. For the present I merely wish to make the point that widely quoted statistics are sometimes used to carry quite different implications from those they really support. The mere fact that 85 per cent of the men interviewed by Kinsey had premarital intercourse does not provide, even on a purely statistical basis, encouragement for the student to go to bed with his date; on the contrary, Kinsey's figures showed that one student out of three does not do so and that students are markedly more concerned about the relational values of sex than the majority of the population.

A second danger in the use of statistical material lies in the failure to take account of the varieties of individual character and sexual needs. Kinsey complained, with good cause, that religious codes have sought unrealistically to impose one standard upon all, despite differences of sexual potential which are partly due to hereditary, glandular, and metabolic factors.[24] But, alas, Kinsey's own work has now led to a new and equally burdensome uniformity of expectation. Christopher Jencks, reviewing Gael Greene's *Sex and the College Girl,* made an astute observation which is as relevant *mutatis mutandis* to the male student as to the coed:

> What has the so-called revolution meant for those too homely, too disagreeable, too sheltered, or too inhibited to participate in the sexual economy? My guess is that they are the real losers as campus mores change. For every suicide brought on by sexual intercourse, there are probably a dozen precipitated by lack of dates; for every psychiatric patient burdened with an unwanted marriage or an unforgotten abortion, there are probably two suffering from the absence of invitations to such disasters.[25]

The man who finds himself less active than his peers is likely to fear for his virility when it is taken for granted that all "normal" people go in for extensive sexual adventure. When it is reported that most young men enjoy three or four orgasms a week, the person who feels no need of so doing is likely to fear that he may be a "prevert" (to use the delightful misnomer of the air-force major in *Dr. Strangelove*) or a sissy. The student who would otherwise restrain himself from the immediate satisfaction of his instinctual drives may be discouraged from the attempt and then suffer agonies of self-reproach simply because he is led to believe that control is impossible.

A few minutes of rational analysis will demonstrate the absurdity of this way of thinking, but all too often rational analysis is the approach least likely to be used when the tyranny of statistics is supposedly bolstered by scientific evidence. In the first place, it should be recognized by now that the flaunting of sexual prowess and achievement is itself commonly a sign of sexual inadequacy or insecurity. The man who feels it necessary to challenge his more retiring fraternity brother into demonstrating his virility by recounting often imaginary tales of conquest is much more likely to be "undersexed." Indeed, this misleading term would be best abandoned. The equation "sexually restrained = undersexed = lacking in virility" is one of the unexamined bits of nonsense in sex lore. Nothing but sheer prejudice could write off all celibate clergy or every man whose sexual outlets are restricted to marriage as lacking in virility or masculinity.

In the second place, the "average" is never, in human affairs, the universal. The statistical median is arrived at by correlating many different examples, including extremes at both ends of the scale. The very idea (and it is only an idea, not a fact, since every individual has his own distinctive worth and cannot be reduced to a figure on a scale) of a norm of sexual activity depends upon the inclusion in the calculation of a considerable proportion of examples who differ radically from the median. Consequently, nobody who values his own independence and uniqueness will or should allow the average to determine what his own behavior will be.

There is a very peculiar inconsistency in *The Playboy Philosophy* in this connection. One of Hefner's most persistent fears is that our society is becoming increasingly and disastrously uniform—a tendency, oddly enough, which the influence of *Playboy,* with its omniscient Advisor ready to tell the inquirer exactly what to wear or drink or drive, would seem to encourage. Nevertheless, the official *credo* is, "We believe wholeheartedly in the Uncommon Man and in his right to be uncommon." [26] Yet I wonder if, in practice, the reader of the magazine gains the impression that this admiration for individuality applies to the sphere of sex? Here, I cannot help feeling, the talk is always of what everybody else is doing. The exception—the man who declares that he has more important things to attend to, the ascetic or the celibate, the virgin or the puritan—is made to feel a dumbbell or a hypocrite. To whom, I wonder, does *The Playboy Philosophy* speak most clearly? To the dedicated scientist, the fearless explorer, the adventurous intellectual, the imaginative artist—or to the comfortable, well-dressed suburban man of those glossy advertisements? Or could it just possibly be that Hefner's ideal Uncommon Man has something in common with Ellis's Successful Seducer?

Can Sexual Desires Be Controlled?

One argument which is very popular with those who advocate the free and uninhibited satisfaction of sexual desires as "natural" is the analogy between sexual need and physical hunger. Hugh Hefner quotes Theodor Reik to show that "it would make as much sense to try to convince us that other natural urges, like thirst or hunger, could be redirected into the accomplishments of cultural achievements, as to suggest that man's basic sex drive could be put to such use." [27] Albert Ellis states dogmatically: "When a young man does, for any considerable period of time, remain *even moderately* (not to mention completely) abstinent, there is every reason to believe that he may do himself considerable harm and that he is practically never likely to do himself any good." [28] The italics are mine, but they draw attention to the implicit conviction that any man who does not gorge himself on sex with considerable frequency is bound for trouble. Just as physical hunger must be satisfied if we are to remain healthy, runs the argument, sexual desire must be satisfied if we are to remain healthy. To make any attempt at direction or control is to attempt the impossible: religious or other restraints can only lead to repression and ultimate disaster. But the analogy deserves more careful examination.

It is clearly very inexact because *all* human beings need a certain minimum intake of sustenance regularly in order to survive physically. The satisfaction of sexual desire consistent with physical or mental health varies (as Kinsey showed) over a much wider range of frequency and regularity. Nevertheless, it is known that men can endure considerable periods without their normal supplies of food without ill effects. Continued restraint in eating habits, as when dieting, has a more or less permanent effect on the individual's need for large quantities of food because the system adapts itself to different conditions. Thus, the analogy, so far as it goes, supports the view that sexual satisfaction can, at least within limits, be controlled or restrained without harm. In other words, the analogy is valid insofar as it reflects the truth that we cannot *ignore* or *repress* our sexual drives without danger; it does nothing to support the view that our sexual activities are beyond our direction and choice. Indeed, one of the most important conclusions from Kinsey's studies is that the forms and types of sexual expression in a whole community can and do change. Unless we assume that *all* Victorians, except the occasional libertine, were seriously neurotic, we must allow that their inhibited sexual lives were relatively satisfying to them—even if such lives would be intolerable today. The fact that the use of prostitutes is much less common among college men today, whereas petting to orgasm is much more common (whatever the cause or the rationale) is proof that we are not bound inevitably to one predetermined pattern of sexual behavior. We are not simply animals controlled by physical instinct to be statistically charted; we are personal beings, able to modify our sexual activities in relation to our self-understanding and our love and respect for other human persons. Indeed, Erich Fromm has observed: "It is not sexual behavior that determines character, but character that determines sexual behavior." [29] Of course, restraint and discipline never come easily to us. The powerful elemental force of sex can very easily burst open the little dykes of direction and control that we construct. It is at this point that Christian churches, with their corporate resources and what a recent author has called "the contagion" of Jesus, can help the student achieve a solution to his dilemma if they will start where he is, without judging him.

The devotee of naturalism is likely at this point to object that I am introducing the discredited idea of sublimation. But this is a term frequently bandied about with little understanding of what it implies. Commonly, it is understood to mean "a conscious decision to avoid the expression and fulfillment of sexual drives and their redirection into some other channel." But this is a great oversimplification. Freud, to whom we owe the term, believed that in the unconscious processes of childhood development, the sexual energy, instead of being repressed as it often is, with disastrous results, is in some cases allowed to find expression in cultural, social, or aesthetic activity. He did not think that the adult could, by conscious determination, divert his sexual drives into nonsexual channels: this attempt he believed to be the cause of much psychological disorder.[30] When Kinsey reported that sublimation was impossible because he had discovered no individuals "whose erotic responses have been reduced or eliminated, *without nervous disturbance,* as a result of an expenditure of energy in utterly nonsexual activities," he was hardly offering any effective repudiation of Freud's position.[31] There are indeed reputable authorities who believe that sublimation offers an effective, conscious therapeutic process, notably the Italian psychotherapist Roberto Assagioli, whose position Havelock Ellis strongly commended.[32] Assagioli points out that sublimation, or transmutation, is an established fact in the experience of many people, including Schopenhauer and Wagner.[33] It is true that this achievement is only possible, as Havelock Ellis pointed out, "for those natures which are of finer than average nervous texture." [34] For most people, indeed, complete sublimation is impossible. But there is no reason to dismiss all lifelong celibates who claim to have achieved it as "undersexed," liars, or uniformly neurotic; maybe none of them chose to tell the Kinsey researchers about it.

But this is beside the point. Let us grant for the moment that those with strong sexual needs cannot permanently ignore them without disaster. Let us grant that the *libido* cannot be redirected into different channels by conscious decision. Let us suppose that those men who abstain from overt sexual activity throughout their lives without emotional disturbance are differently constituted—though not necessarily less manly—from the rest. It is an ignorant but popular trick to suppose that by thus rejecting the possibility of complete sublimation, one has shown that any kind of partial or temporary restraint is damaging or undesirable. Only if the sexual instincts are repudiated, perverted, or strictly repressed does damage arise. "There seems no ground," wrote Havelock Ellis, "to believe that any serious psychosis or neurosis is caused by sexual abstinence alone in congenitally sound persons." [35] The idea that "abstinence for any long period of time may impair one's capacities for subsequent performance" is an entirely unproven teenage myth according to Kinsey.[36] Although an overscrupulous attempt to control *all* sexual outlets after puberty may indeed be damaging, to make some responsible choice between, say, masturbation and using a prostitute is surely a mark of maturity. To avoid intercourse because one is unable to face the reality of one's sexuality, or because of the prohibition of an oversevere superego is, indeed, to be "abnormal"—to be emotionally sick. But to do so because one looks forward to marriage and wishes to preserve that high joy for one particular girl and one particular time is not only an open possibility—it is a mark of fully developed personal freedom. The man who subordinates every other concern or interest to the satisfaction of sexual desire is perhaps doing what comes naturally to him as an animal, but he is hardly doing what is natural for him as a responsible human being.

Of course, the temporary denial of the immediate satisfaction of sexual desire is justified only in the interests of a greater good. But the traditional religious assumption that the greater good consists in a heavenly reward or the achievement of "spiritual" freedom from the demands of the flesh no longer carries conviction. We need a new definition of what is natural for us as human beings.

A New Definition of the Natural

Instead of measuring our humanity by the refined dualism of the medieval monastery or the statistical uniformity of the average man, we must consider its unique qualities and fulfill our sexuality within this context. Havelock Ellis made the following comment on the traditional view that coitus is justified only for procreation, but it applies with equal force to those who argue that it is justified for pleasure alone:

In determining what is natural for man, we are not entitled to consider the practice of the animals belonging to remote genera. We have to consider the general practice of the human species, which by no means shows so narrowly exclusive an aim in procreation. . . . We are quite justified in departing, if we think fit, from the habits of the lower races. Certainly, the sexual organs were developed for procreation, not for the sexual gratification of the individual; certainly also the hands were developed to serve nutrition, not to play on the piano or the violin. But if the individual can find joy and inspiration in using his organs for ends they were not made for, he is following a course of action which, whether or not we choose to call it "natural," is perfectly justifiable and moral. . . . Human art legitimately comes into human activities, but it introduces no real conflict with Nature.[37]

In the previous chapter, I argued that love alone can give to sex its full meaning, and I suggested that in the life of Jesus we can find epitomized that complete self-giving of which every experience of "true love" is a partial reflection. We noted then that Jesus did not share the later Christian aversion to sex because he was free of that dualism which sets the spirit over against the body—just as he was free of the modern dualism which sets the body over against the spirit. His conception of what is natural for man differs from either of the views examined in this chapter. He saw man in his wholeness (and his sexuality) as a child of God, invested with unique capacities for faith and love. He did not call upon us to deny our sexuality, to castigate our bodies, to destroy our self-respect. He did not ask us to love our neighbors *instead of* ourselves—nor did he cease to be, in the extremity of his love, a complete and individual man. But, on the other hand, he did not suppose that man could come to maturity in isolation, dedicated to his own pleasure and self-interest. For Jesus the natural, true, human life requires that we love our neighbor *as ourselves.* We are not doing what comes naturally if we fail to respect the nature of others. As John Macmurray wrote in a book recently republished as a paperback: "The integrity of persons is inviolable. You shall not use a person for your own ends, or indeed for any ends, individual or social. To use another person is to violate his personality by making an object of him; and in violating the integrity of another, you violate your own." [38]

We may redefine the natural, therefore, in terms of unique potentiality for personal relationships and love. The man who allows himself to be guided by immediate desire and self-interest is not "doing what comes naturally," he is falling below the level of *human* nature. To trivialize sex by using another person's body for my passing pleasure is not only to wrong that individual; it is to reduce my own humanity to the level of the beasts. Anthony Storr has written: "The study of sexual deviation is very largely the study of sex divorced from love." [39] I close this chapter with a striking comment, from his book *Sexual Deviation,* which may serve as a text upon which the more practical discussions of the following chapters are based:

> Sexual intercourse may be said to be one aspect, perhaps the most basic and most important aspect, of a relationship between persons. In ideally mature form it is a relationship between a man and a woman in which giving and taking is equal, and in which the genitals are the most important channel through which love is expressed and received. It is one of the most natural, and certainly the most rewarding and the most life-enhancing of all human experiences. It is also the only one which both has a completely satisfying ending and yet can be endlessly repeated. Not even the greatest works of literature and music can stand such iteration. But this wonderfully enriching experience is only possible when the two people concerned have achieved a relationship in which, at least during the actual process of love-making, each is able to confront the other exactly as they are, with no reserves and no pretences, and in which there is no admixture of childish dependence or fear.[40]

7 SEX—ALL ALONE

Almost every male college student has nocturnal emissions, or "wet dreams," and for a great many boys this experience is initially both shameful and frightening.[1] Sometimes the uninstructed adolescent confuses the experience with bed-wetting and is appalled at his supposed lack of continence. He frequently remembers, on waking, that he has been dreaming and that the dream has involved an exciting physical relationship with a girl (usually unidentifiable) of a kind which he knows is disapproved of by his parents and teachers.[2] He has probably been taught from infancy that his penis is objectionable and erection disgusting. The fact that his mother usually makes no comment on the stained sheet increases the sense of involvement in something unmentionable yet at the same time pleasurable and satisfying. Thus, society helps to initiate him into its confused attitude toward sexuality. For, although this sexual outlet is the only one officially accepted as permissible for the unmarried man, on the scientifically questionable ground that it is the result of purely physical pressure on the reproductive glands, the lack of adequate preparation or explanation makes it, too, a source of anxiety.[3] From the first, sexuality is thus identified with secrecy, adult embarrassment, and a sense of guilt. What the growing boy finds fascinating and wants to understand is somehow marked as closed to inspection. What he knows instinctively to be part of his budding manhood is vaguely suspect. When his curiosity is aroused, he finds he cannot obtain clear and honest answers in this sphere, however ready his elders may be to impart knowledge on every other subject.

When he continues to explore these new and exciting potentialities, and discovers that he can achieve orgasm through the manual stimulation of his genitals, the young adolescent almost certainly encounters positive objection and violent rebuke. Although ninety-six out of every hundred college-level males practice masturbation, almost as high a percentage as those experiencing nocturnal emission, this outlet is explicitly condemned by the official mores of our society.[4]

The Disaster of Official Condemnation

It is, in fact, no less inevitable and no less a part of the psychophysical development of adolescence than is nocturnal emission, but it has been the subject of excessive and entirely irrational condemnation by the churches. A recent report, *Sex and the College Student,* formulated by the Committee on the College Student of the Group for the Advancement of Psychiatry, states:

> Masturbation serves . . . a variety of purposes including different emotional needs at different stages of development for each person. The physical act is importantly linked with conscious and unconscious fantasy. Altogether, in addition to the simple discharge of sexual tension, masturbation serves such purposes as the reduction of anxiety, expression of hostility, fantasying of sexual experimentation, assertion of sexual identity in anticipation or recall.[5]

Yet Catholic clergy often regard it as one of the more serious sins, and until very recently most Protestant churches taught that "self-abuse" was both physically and spiritually destructive. An Anglican Archdeacon recently wrote in a letter to *Prism*: "Every confessor must know how immensely in character young people have grown who have thrown off this habit."[6] Exaggerated feelings of guilt are thus developed by the great majority of young men brought up within the Christian tradition—with the result that any satisfactory adjustment to mature sexuality is made extremely difficult for them.[7] Frequently, the outcome is the total and equally distorted rejection of all the traditional religious ideals of restraint and chastity, the confusion of lust and love, and capitulation to the new tyranny of statistics.

The clergy, however, are by no means alone to blame for this situation. The Boy Scout Manual, as late as 1945, stated: "It is a bad habit. It should be fought against. . . . It is something to keep away from." [8] In 1948 Kinsey found that the Naval Academy at Annapolis rejected candidates who showed "evidence of masturbation"—whatever that means.[9]

The words of the unofficial report *Towards a Quaker View of Sex,* published in England in 1963, could equally apply to the present situation in the United States:

Masturbation is still avoided as a subject, both by adolescents and by those whom they might consult. Often the only literature available is that which unfortunately discusses the subject under the name of "self-abuse." It is difficult to exaggerate the suffering induced by the sense of guilt and disgrace, the mental conflict and remorse that so commonly invest this intimate matter. How rarely is it ever dealt with by parent or teacher, priest or doctor, except in ways destined only to increase the suffering. Much would be saved even by the simple acknowledgment that masturbation is the common experience of the great majority of men at some times, if not of so large a proportion of women.[10]

Guilt about sex and, in particular, about masturbation is so deeply rooted in our culture that no amount of rational discussion can altogether dispel it. Any man who feels that he must, because of the teaching of his church, avoid masturbation would be foolish to run counter to a deeply established religious prohibition. Even the most vigorous exponents of the "natural" view of masturbation recognize that it can have significant psychological consequences when practiced by those whose consciences disallow it, though this fact does not necessarily support the traditional view that guilt is inherent in the act itself.[11] To argue, as Canon Herbert Waddams does in a recent work, that masturbation should be avoided because it produces "guilt feelings which have serious secondary effects" is to beg the question.[12] Is the uneasy conscience due to the inherent perversity of masturbation or is it largely or entirely the product of our religious and cultural ethos? What we know of the sexual customs of some primitive peoples suggests the latter.[13] Nevertheless, where profound guilt feelings are associated with masturbation, they must be respected unless or until a new understanding of the practice and its significance is achieved. All that can be done here is to remind anyone so troubled that he is *not* the only man in his class or his church to indulge in "the solitary vice," and to analyze the arguments traditionally advanced to discourage it.

The Supposed Physical Effects

The most effective and most popular argument for the past two centuries, since Hume wrote his *Onanism: or a Treatise upon the Disorders Produced by Masturbation,* in 1766, has been to the effect that it causes physical or mental sickness. J. H. Kellogg, in *Plain Facts for Old and Young* (1879), attributed almost every imaginable disorder to masturbation. His list of symptoms included lassitude, sleeplessness, bashfulness, unnatural boldness, mock piety, confusion of ideas, round shoulders, weak backs, paralysis, the use of tobacco, moist hands, palpitation of the heart, hysteria, epilepsy, bed-wetting, impotence, dyspepsia, cancer, insanity, and suicide.[14] His suggested cures included perpetual watching of the subject, bandaging the parts, covering the organs with a cage, and circumcision. However, it is a mistake to suppose that only cranks and prudes shared this view in the nineteenth century. Krafft-Ebing, in his recently republished *Psychopathia Sexualis,* took it for granted that nervous disease and insanity result from masturbation. Freud believed that continual masturbation would weaken the child's capacities for education.[15] Even Havelock Ellis thought that "any excess in solitary self-excitement" could affect the skin, digestion, and circulation.[16]

Nowadays, however, it is widely accepted that the physical or psychic effects of masturbation are not necessarily different from those of any other sexual activity. It may, indeed, be a contributing factor in emotional disorder when practiced by those whose religious convictions forbid it. It is a common symptom of such psychosexual deviation as anal eroticism, exhibitionism, and voyeurism.[17] It is practiced without inhibitions or privacy by people who are insane or mentally retarded, and it is from this association that many misconceptions have arisen. But, in itself, masturbation is almost certainly entirely harmless in its effects on the human body or the human mind.

There is no evidence to support the view, held even by Havelock Ellis, that masturbation makes a normal later adjustment to heterosexual relations difficult.[18] Kinsey found a specific correlation in women between premarital masturbation and the early achievement of orgasm in marital coitus.[19] Where any such difficulty does occur, it is due to some psychological disorder of which masturbation may, indeed, be a symptom. The exclusive use of masturbation for sexual expression may reflect a failure to enter into personal relations, or a refusal to accept the reality of one's sexuality. A persistent preference for masturbation in adult life, when normal heterosexual relations are possible—for example, in marriage—may well be indicative of neurosis. Masturbation accompanied by nothing but homosexual fantasies may be symptomatic of homosexual tendencies, though by no means necessarily of permanent inversion. Masturbatory fantasies of a sadomasochistic type call for psychiatric treatment. But the *absence* of any fantasy or daydream, far from indicating that the act is less perverse as many religious authorities claim, may reflect a more profound narcissism, since masturbation is then expressive of a purely self-directed mechanical pleasure.[20]

Of these possibilities, however, three things must be said. First, they involve a very small minority of those who masturbate, since 96 per cent of young men do so, and the great majority are not seriously neurotic. Second, within the limits of the student age group, any of these phenomena may be found without their reflecting any profound psychological problem. One man in four, for example, does not engage in fantasy during masturbation; but the great majority of these are quite capable of heterosexual love. Finally, if these symptoms persist in adult life, professional help directed toward curing the underlying condition should be sought. The mere cessation of masturbation, even when possible, will not alleviate the problem and may well exacerbate it.

When writers continue to buttress their religious objections to masturbation with the threat of physical or emotional sickness, they are therefore confusing the issue. If the practice as such is to be rejected, it must be on other grounds. When two Roman Catholic authorities write, as recently as 1959, that masturbation "can be linked to depression, insecurity, a lack of confidence in self, difficulties at school, a lack of affection in the home . . . , above all, an inability to give sex and love their proper and proportionate place in healthy emotional life," they are invoking sanctions which are without support in fact.[21] When Canon Waddams states that masturbation sometimes induces neuroses in young people, he is confusing the consequences of religious scruples with the consequences of the practice itself.[22]

The extent to which ungrounded fears of harm resulting from masturbation still influence student thinking is astonishing. The Kronhausens found that a number of the men they interviewed suffered from fear of losing their hair, or breaking out in pimples, or going blind, or approaching insanity as a result of masturbation. In some cases these fears were the result of specific warnings given by supposedly enlightened parents! [23] It is the excessive condemnation of the practice, given apparent force by such unwarranted threats, that produces the damage. The young man finds it physically impossible to suppress his inevitable sexual curiosity and then suffers untold guilt and fear. Or he represses the sexual urge and lays up trouble for the future in the form of true neurosis. If masturbation were accepted as a natural phenomenon of adolescence, no more reprehensible than wet dreams or the onset of menstruation in girls, it would never play a significant part in most men's lives. To condemn it as wicked and sinful is as stupid as to punish a baby for crying when it is hungry or a child for climbing trees. It is symptomatic of a healthy desire for sexual experience and of normal adolescent virility. It is the concentration of moral effort on the irrelevant and virtually impossible task of damming up a basic urge that produces anxiety and detracts attention from more important and worth-while concerns.

There are, however, other arguments upon which religious prohibition can be based, and these would remain valid and would indeed be more compelling (to those convinced by them) if they were clearly dissociated from unjustified threats of physical or emotional disorders.

A Superstitious Reverence for Semen

Catholic objections still depend to a large extent upon what Sherwin Bailey has called "a superstitious reverence for semen, which had its origin in antiquity." [24] The early fathers of the church shared the current medical assumption that the embryo at conception was concocted from semen and menstrual fluid, the woman being "little more than a well-equipped incubator." [25] The semen was therefore thought to be "almost human" and its "wastage" a form of mass murder. This is the real reason why our society has been and still is far more severe in its attitude toward male homosexuals than toward lesbians, whose sexual intimacies involve no such loss of embryonic life.[26]

Such a view is, however, extremely difficult to maintain today. In the first place, we now understand that the female ovum plays a decisive and positive role in the production of the embryo. Without it the male contribution is anything but human. Indeed, even St. Thomas Aquinas decided that the distinctively human soul was only added to the embryo on the fortieth day of pregnancy in the case of boys and the eightieth in that of girls.[27] Second, it is now known that every normal ejaculation of semen contains several hundred million sperms, any one of which can lead to conception. This is mass murder with a vengeance! But it also suggests that the Almighty is not as anxiously careful with his provision of potential infants as many of his representatives have claimed. When it is remembered that millions of sperms are "wasted" every time a man has a wet dream, or every time a married couple has coitus in the safe period—let alone when other contraceptives are used—the absurdity of the argument is obvious. It originated in a time when underpopulation was a serious problem. Lewinsohn suggests that sexual abstinence "did more than excess to bring about the downfall of Rome"; and the Christian Church, with its emphasis upon virginity and monogamy, found it necessary to its own survival to discourage any sexual activity, from *coitus interruptus* to masturbation, which might provide people with satisfaction but would deny them offspring.[28] In an age in which even the Catholic Church is moving toward the acceptance of some forms of birth control, in the face of the population explosion, there are few to whom this objection to masturbation carries any conviction.

I think that we can understand, even if we do not appreciate, the exaggerated horror of masturbation in medieval clerical thinking if we recognize the fact that this practice represented to the most conscientious and sincere theological authorities of the time the only—and therefore the most burdensome—threat to their vows of chastity. We know from the penitentials, which provided guidance for confessors and set the appropriate penance for every imaginable infringement of the medieval ethical code, that it was often felt necessary to provide separately for the discipline of clergy who engaged in masturbation. It must be remembered that the imposition of celibacy on all clergy was only made effective by Rome in the twelfth century, and that opposition to the universal rule in the Western Church was strong until that time. Once imposed, however, it was inevitable that many men who should have heeded St. Paul's dictum that it is "better to marry than burn" found themselves in an impossible position. For a great many, ordination was the only possible path to education and knowledge. Being ignorant of the dynamics of sexual energy, they assumed that prayer and discipline could enable them to avoid all forms of sexual outlet.

We all know, however, that large numbers failed to maintain chastity. Stories of clerical immorality are often exaggerated because the canon law of the time stigmatized as "incontinent" many a priest who was in fact living honorably—though illegally—with a woman who was his wife in all but name.[29] Nevertheless, the evidence shows that for a considerable proportion of the clergy (who numbered one in thirteen of the male population in the thirteenth century), the yoke of celibacy proved too heavy. G. Rattray Taylor's statement that homosexual practices were "above all the failing of the priesthood" is not supported by the facts, but it was inevitable that liaisons between monks occurred.[30] Others, in all likelihood being of a different metabolic or psychic constitution, never found the need of any other sexual outlet besides nocturnal emission, for which the penitentials provided very minor penalties.

It is not an unreasonable assumption that many of the most sincere and disciplined of the medieval clergy, who maintained their vows unbroken as regards overt sexual relations with women or other men, found it impossible to abstain from masturbation. Being unaware of the profundity and complexity of sex in human nature, and finding themselves compelled to seek relief in a practice which (unlike nocturnal emission) appeared to be within the control of reason and will, they felt obliged to treat this disturbing failure with special seriousness. The responsible priest or monk—the man who was most likely to influence the formation of codes of behavior for clergy and laity—disapproved of adultery or fornication; but they were not his temptation—those dangers he could and did avoid merely by shutting himself off from women. On the other hand, masturbation was not only a temptation but a common occasion for the defilement of his priestly vocation. This he hated; and partly to punish himself, partly to help himself avoid another fall, he attached to it a penalty altogether too severe even by the harsh standards of that day. Thus, St. Thomas Aquinas regarded

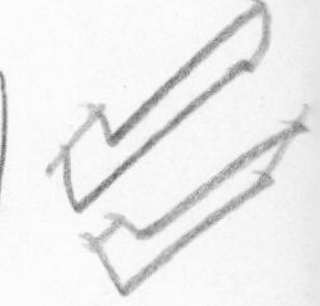

masturbation as worse than incest, adultery, rape, or fornication—despite the fact that these were assumed to involve the degradation of another person as well as the perpetrator.[31]

For Protestants, of course, the rulings of medieval monks are hardly decisive—though their assumptions still largely determine, in practice, the sexual codes of the Reformed Churches. Here, the court of appeal is the account of the sin of Onan in Genesis 38; indeed, "onanism" has become a technical term for masturbation. According to the ancient story, Onan was required to take the place of his dead brother, Er, and to raise up children in his place through intercourse with his widow. This he refused to do. Instead, he spilled the semen on the ground, and was slain by Yahweh, the God of Israel. For centuries the story of the divine judgment on Onan proved an effective instrument for terrifying young men, and was productive of immeasurable anguish and untold neurosis. Today, however, it is almost universally agreed by Protestant scholars that the "sin" of Onan consisted in his failure to fulfill his responsibility to his dead brother.[32] His method of so doing was probably *coitus interruptus* rather than masturbation. But even if the Bible did contain a formal condemnation of masturbation, this would not necessarily require even the devout Christian to accept its estimate of the seriousness of the act. The Old Testament also condemns the eating of pork. It requires that witches be stoned and homosexual acts punished by death. According to the Mosaic law, anyone who curses his parents is to be executed, and those who have intercourse during menstruation are to be cut off from the people. After a wet dream, a man must separate himself from society and only return to the community after sundown, and if he has intercourse with a woman, she also is unclean for a full day.[33] No Christian Church has ever taken these regulations *au pied de la lettre,* and there is absolutely no reason—other than the inbred and irrational antisexualism which has plagued Christian thought—why masturbation should be condemned on the basis of the biblical story of Onan.

An Unavoidable Dissatisfaction

The alternative to moral condemnation is not, however, unqualified enthusiasm. I have no wish to be associated with the unsavory Dr. Krankeit, who, in that altogether unsubtle spoof on pornography, *Candy,* argues that heterosexual love is the root of all neurosis and advocates masturbation as "the only sex-mode that permits complete fulfillment and mental health." [34] I suspect that a certain degree of dissatisfaction and frustration, which will frequently take the form of guilt feelings, is inseparable from the practice of masturbation, at least after the initial stage of adolescent exploration and experimentation. Anthony Storr suggests that a certain degree of sexual guilt, in connection with the incest taboo, may have its advantages since it encourages the young person to seek others of his own age to provide the understanding which parents cannot give.[35] I suggest that the same may be true of masturbation, and the sense of guilt, of failure to achieve perfection, may be the necessary challenge to move on to the fuller realization of sexuality in mutual love with another person. Havelock Ellis pointed out the following:

> The sexual orgasm is normally bound up with a mass of powerful emotions aroused by a person of the opposite sex. It is in the joy caused by the play of these emotions, as well as in the discharge of the sexual orgasm, that the satisfaction of coitus resides. In the absence of the desired partner the orgasm, whatever relief it may give, must be followed by a sense of dissatisfaction, perhaps of depression, even of exhaustion, often of shame and remorse.[36]

The natural development of the physical organism would be to enter into the full sexual experience of intercourse in the early teens; the equally natural demands of human responsibility and advanced civilization make this impossible. Freud was surely right in seeing that masturbation has become a temporary symptom of the neurosis inseparable from the complex structure of human life—though one which normally gives place to sexual maturity and health if it is not compounded by exaggerated guilt feelings. Masturbation is therefore an escape valve, however inadequate in itself, which makes possible the survival of our society without the universal debasement of heterosexual intercourse to the level of purely animal satisfaction. Many students find it necessary to masturbate after a date. Society, as we have seen, has established a cultural and economic milieu in which their sexual appetites are whetted by innumerable stimulants and their physical contact with girls encouraged from the preteens on. Would it be better, as some imply, for them to press their attentions on unready girls, or, if the girl is ready, to engage mutually in the full sex act without the depths of personal relationship which it properly expresses? Since there is evidence that advanced sexual arousal without relief in orgasm may result in serious nervous strain,[37] I would argue that masturbation is more consistent with the good of the persons concerned. The view often expressed [38] that coitus in *any* circumstances is more natural than masturbation surely ignores the question of personal responsibility for the girl involved. It is true that for the man intercourse is usually more satisfying physically; but I have been arguing for a view of sex which rejects the identification of the natural and the physically pleasurable on the human level. It seems to me that the Christian should be able to accept this outlet thankfully in a world in which God is creating free beings with their origins in the animal world and their destiny in free self-giving love. The proper response of the man who finds masturbation helpful, though also frustrating and unsatisfying, is not anxious fear of God's judgment, but a humble acceptance of his provision of this temporary substitute for the full joys of sexual union.

Unfortunately, it is not uncommon for people who regard themselves as emancipated from religious convention to suffer under another kind of anxiety associated with masturbation. Frequently, physicians and some psychiatrists advise their patients that masturbation is legitimate and harmless "if you don't do it too often," and then fail to give any indication as to what is or is not excessive. The result often is that the boy is as much terrified by the fear of exceeding an undefined limit as he was previously by a blanket condemnation. The fact is, however, that sexual activity is self-correcting, and when the limit of physiological endurance is reached (a limit which varies greatly with the individual), there is no more erotic response. There is no way in which the mere physical act of masturbating can result in permanent damage to the system; before that can occur the neurological reflexes will have ceased to operate, and it will be literally impossible to continue.[39] Any sexual arousal followed by orgasm results in a temporary loss of energy, but this effect is readily corrected by a night's sleep. The man who needs to be physically or mentally alert will suffer more from spending a broken night fighting off the desire than he will if he masturbates and enjoys a sound sleep. To concentrate one's attention on avoiding masturbation is to divert psychic and spiritual resources into entirely secondary, negative, and probably unsuccessful activity. To accept it as a necessary release of tension is to free the self for positive and constructive interests, among which masturbation will find its proper, minor, and temporary place.

8 SEX—ALL MALE

"One day a good-looking young student sat in my office, wringing his hands, and trying to make his difficult confession. He finally came out with what was to him, and what would be to most people in our culture, a terrible thing—he had allowed another individual to perform fellatio on him. Now he felt himself to be morally degenerate and a pervert of the worst type. He saw his future ruined, his chances dim of ever again leading a 'normal' life—and he thought the best way out might be to prove that he was a man by getting married posthaste!" [1]

This type of situation, described by Phyllis Kronhausen, is familiar to every chaplain, counsellor, or dean who deals with students. For a considerable number of men in college, the dilemma of sex consists in discovering whether their future lies in a normal heterosexual development, or whether they must identify themselves with the subculture of the homosexual world. Both the glittering and increasingly publicized attractions of that way of life and the prejudiced misunderstanding generally prevailing in our society tend to encourage or force a young man with any homosexual experience into a path which may be by no means inevitable.

It is impossible to deal adequately in one chapter with the whole range of issues involved in homosexuality, but the following propositions need to be emphasized and widely recognized if the student is to avoid unnecessary anxiety and possible disaster.

First, nobody in his senses will accept a homosexual way of life if he can avoid it. Second, a large number of men who are not fundamentally or even exceptionally homosexual in their orientation have adult homosexual experiences. Third, no one within the normal student age range has reason to conclude that his homosexual urges, however strong, are either basic or permanent.

Popular Misconceptions

Before we elaborate on these propositions, however, it is necessary to correct some misconceptions about homosexuality, which persist despite the greatly increased literature on the subject. Many people find the matter almost impossible to discuss rationally because of a deeply ingrained sense of aesthetic disgust about the physical aspects of homosexuality. Many take it for granted that homosexuals are all "sodomites," who find sexual relief through anal intercourse; but this is quite untrue. The report *Towards a Quaker View of Sex* expresses the conviction that "It may well be in fact more common among married people than between homosexual partners: and there is no evidence that homosexuals are drawn to sodomy more than others." [2]

The great majority of homosexuals obtain their satisfaction from manual petting or oral-genital contacts, which are widely accepted in the heterosexual world, and which frequently form the preliminary to coitus for a man and a woman. There is certainly no rational ground for regarding all homosexual body contacts as any more disgusting than those of normal people. As a matter of fact, the physical acts of sex are almost always unattractive to the onlooker. In my experience the reaction of students to "skin flicks" is largely one of disgust—although they feel it necessary to demonstrate their maturity by viewing them. As Havelock Ellis remarked, "Not even the most recognized methods of sexual intercourse can well be described as 'aesthetic.' It is not understood that here, amid the most intimate mysteries of love, we are in a region where the cold and abstract viewpoints either of science or of aesthetics are out of place unless qualified by more specially human emotions." [3]

It must also be pointed out that the grotesque exhibitionism of "fairies," or "queens," who dress themselves up in women's clothes and ape female mannerisms is neither characteristic of, nor generally appreciated by, homosexuals. One of the most articulate and respected spokesmen for the homosexual world, Donald Webster Cory, has recently pointed out, "The 'fairy' or the 'nellie' gets spurned by most homosexuals, not only because of the social stigma attached to being seen with him, but because the gay guy is looking for a man, not for a woman." [4]

The fact that men with thoroughly heterosexual orientation sometimes have the same tendency to cross-sex identification suggests that the causes may be quite different from those underlying homosexuality.[5] Much of the exaggerated publicity given to the more extreme forms of sexual perversion, such as sadomasochism, practiced by a small percentage of homosexuals, is due to the fact that until very recently the subject was taboo in the popular press.

When John Rechy's repetitious and turgid *City of Night* appeared in 1963, a reviewer in *The New York Times* remarked, "This novel would surely not have been published as little as five years ago." [6] In fact, it would not be very difficult to find heterosexual parallels to the pathetic stories of grasping loneliness and personal depravity described by Rechy in that nightmare tour of the United States. These, however, are neither newsworthy nor comforting to the prejudices of the majority. It is the homosexual deviate, whose excesses can be attributed by osmosis to the whole group, who provides the convenient subject of curiosity and contempt for a society which has so miserably failed to come to terms with its own sexuality. Dr. Sherwin Bailey, at the conclusion of his important study *Homosexuality and the Western Christian Tradition,* points out that our society "instead of addressing itself energetically to the reform of all that is amiss in its sexual life and ideas . . . has attempted to relieve its sense of guilt by turning upon the male homosexual as a convenient scapegoat." [7]

Finally, it must be said that homosexuals are not the serious menace to society that they are frequently supposed to be. Dr. D. J. West, perhaps the leading British authority in this field, writes, "The possession of homosexual inclinations no more defines a man's character than the possession of a nervous twitch.

. . . Homosexuals are merely a collection of ordinary human beings, neither specially gifted nor specially evil, who react in different ways to their common problem."[8] Because of the unwarranted publicity often given to cases in which homosexuals are involved, there is a widespread impression that they are a particular menace to young children. But there is no clear evidence that homosexuals are more prone than heterosexuals to molest children.

Of course, homosexuals include men with criminal tendencies, and, insofar as the condition is symptomatic of neurotic or psychotic disturbance, it is probable that a larger percentage of homosexuals than of heterosexuals becomes involved in antisocial acts or fails to contribute positively to the common good. But homosexuality in itself is not necessarily socially destructive. Many men who have contributed significantly to our understanding in philosophy, politics, and the arts have been homosexuals. Leonardo, Michelangelo, Tchaikovsky, Walt Whitman, André Gide, and Marcel Proust (not to mention the unfortunate Oscar Wilde) are frequently named in this connection.

There can be little doubt that the present repressive laws against homosexuals quite unfairly penalize a minority group and cause unnecessary and untold pain and fear to many men who are otherwise law-abiding and responsible citizens. Indeed, these laws considerably increase criminal activity by the opportunities they offer for blackmail; and by giving the homosexual community the character of a persecuted minority, they encourage the more aggressive and objectionable members of that community. It is noteworthy that the American Law Institute issued a Model Penal Code in 1955 which recommended that private homosexual acts between consenting adults should be excluded from the criminal law, since "no harm to the secular interests of the community is involved . . . , and there is the fundamental question of the protection to which every individual is entitled against state interference in his personal affairs when he is not hurting others."[9] In England, as is well known, the Wolfenden Report made a similar proposal two years later, and in May, 1965, the House of Lords approved a bill embodying the reform, which was later rejected by only a small minority in the Commons.[10] What is not so well known is that both the Church of England and the Roman Catholics in England supported this proposed change in the law.[11]

The Sodom and Gomorrah Complex

Of course, the churches do not by this endorsement of a more liberal legal policy imply that they no longer regard homosexual activities as "unnatural" and sinful. In the Christian tradition, homosexual acts have generally been regarded as especially detestable, though the assumption that homosexuals were the object of particularly vicious ecclesiastical condemnation or the subject of obsessive concern in the Middle Ages is without foundation in fact.[12] The source of this abhorrence, as with the revulsion against masturbation, lay in the current reverence for male seed, the immediacy of the temptation to celibate monks, and another misinterpretation of an Old Testament story. The technical term "sodomy," often used indiscriminately to cover all homosexual acts, was derived from Genesis 19, according to which the city of Sodom, with its neighbor Gomorrah, was destroyed by Yahweh with fire and brimstone. The occasion for this terrible judgment was said to have been the demand made by the inhabitants of Sodom that Lot should hand over to them two men (supposedly angels in disguise) who were guests in his house. Later biblical references to homosexuality make no mention of this story until the very late New Testament epistles of II Peter and Jude, but it was assumed in Jewish circles from the second century B.C. that the reason for the divine wrath was the intention to engage in homosexual activity.

Thus, as with the story of Onan, a dramatic incident provided the means of impressing both Christians and Jews with the heinous character of this particular sin, and all sorts of disasters have been attributed to God's vengeance on those so perverted. But recently Sherwin Bailey has argued persuasively that this interpretation is false to the story and that it was inspired by Jewish "antagonism to the Hellenistic way of life and its exponents, and by contempt for the basest features of Greek sexual immorality." [13] The unqualified condemnation of homosexuals can no longer be justified on the grounds that a natural catastrophe in the remote past once and for all revealed God's will.[14]

As a matter of fact, moral theologians have usually been careful to avoid any blanket condemnation of homosexuals as such, since this would involve singling out some members of the human race as specially evil because of a condition that they have not freely chosen. Since St. Augustine, it has been widely held by orthodox theologians that there is nothing absurd in believing that the *whole* human race is properly liable to damnation for a condition brought on it by another (i.e., Adam); but some inherent respect for the processes of rational moral judgment has generally led the church to distinguish between culpable homosexual *acts* and the nonculpable homosexual *condition*. Thus, when Dr. Geoffrey Fisher, then Archbishop of Canterbury, made his oft-quoted statement to the effect that "homosexual indulgence is a shameful vice and a grievous sin from which deliverance is to be sought by every means," he was careful, though hardly overcareful, to distinguish between the condition and the indulgent acts.[15] On the other hand, when the authors of the Revised Standard Version translated I Corinthians 6:9 to represent St. Paul as denying homosexuals, as a class, from participation in the kingdom of God, they were guilty both of bad theology and of bad linguistics. For the Greek text of this verse speaks of those who engage in homosexual *practices*—and, indeed, the reference may be not to established homosexuals, but to dissolute heterosexuals.[16]

Nevertheless, St. Paul here and elsewhere condemns all homosexual acts without differentiation, and he was followed in this by the early church fathers.[17] We must remember that he and they were entirely ignorant of the causes and nature of homosexuality, and their basic suspicion of all sexuality colored their attitude to any physical expression of love outside the narrowest marital limits. As the Quaker report points out, St. Paul seems to have shared the "prairie fire" view of homosexual conduct, according to which men would automatically turn to it in preference to heterosexual satisfaction if it were permitted.[18] One recent correspondent in *Prism* commented: "I'm not sure that any New Testament writer would approve of us even kissing our mother. Wouldn't that be aberration too?" [19] Certainly, most of our generally accepted forms of precoital sexual play would have been regarded by St. Jerome and his contemporaries as extremely perverse.

This is not to urge that the church can or should abandon its position entirely. It must witness to the inadequacy and imperfection of the homosexual condition and call upon its members to abstain from the satisfaction of physical needs through the purely promiscuous use of other human persons. Yet it surely needs to make far clearer than is usually apparent that it welcomes to its fellowship those with homosexual tendencies; and in the light of modern knowledge, it must re-examine the traditional dismissal of all homosexual relationships as intrinsically evil. Happily, there are signs that such a reassessment is already under way.

A New Religious Approach

Sherwin Bailey's book *Homosexuality and the Western Christian Tradition,* to which reference has already been made, was a milestone in the scholarly and sympathetic study of the subject. He concluded by drawing attention to the inconsistency of treating homosexual acts between men more severely than heterosexual immorality, and to the absurdity of maintaining that the practicing male homosexual does more harm than the man who seduces another's wife and breaks up a marriage.[20]

The Rev. Robert W. Wood, in *Christ and the Homosexual,* has argued with some logic that where homosexual relationships are permanent and profound, they contain an element of integrity and moral worth—though his approach suffers from a too-easy acceptance of the thesis that homosexuality is incurable and inevitable. Finally, the controversial essay *Towards a Quaker View of Sex,* which was hailed by the London *Observer* as "far and away the best study yet produced by any religious group," [21] had this to say:

> Surely it is the nature and quality of a relationship that matters: one must not judge it by its outward appearance but by its inner worth. Homosexual affection can be as selfless as heterosexual affection, and therefore we cannot see that it is in some way morally worse. Homosexual affection may of course be an emotion which some find aesthetically disgusting, but one cannot base Christian morality on a capacity for such disgust. Neither are we happy with the thought that all homosexual behaviour is sinful: motive and circumstances degrade or ennoble any act.[22]

The Quaker report seems to me to suffer by minimizing the distortion of the person which underlies any permanent homosexual fixation. To say that "one should no more deplore homosexuality than left-handedness" is about as silly as saying that one should no more deplore the fact that a child is a cretin than that he has a squint.[23] Moreover, the Quaker report fails to discuss at all adequately the role of physical intimacy in the more mature and ennobling homosexual relationship. It is noteworthy that Havelock Ellis believed this form of sexuality to be particularly amenable to sublimation.[24] And most significant of all, to my mind, is Donald Webster Cory's observation that "we also have a great deal of nonsexual love, or highly affection-laden relationships that homosexuals establish among themselves—loves that are person to person, but devoid of physical contact. . . . *Numerous homosexual relationships are either genital or love contacts, but seldom a combination of both.*" [25]

There are obviously major questions here still unexamined; but it is clear that Christians are beginning to take a more penetrating and humane look at the homosexual picture.

No Truly Happy Homosexuals

This clearing of the ground has been important because any decision that the student is to make about this subject can only be made rationally if the facts are known and the deeply rooted prejudices of our society corrected. We can now return to the first of the propositions stated in the opening of this chapter: *nobody in his senses will accept a homosexual way of life if he can avoid it*. Despite everything that has been said above and everything that may be said by homosexual apologists concerned to acquire the respect and toleration of society, the student who fears he may be homosexual or who is attracted by the gay life should explore every avenue to achieve normal heterosexual capacities and relationships. Despite the claim that homosexuality is the wave of the future, or, as one homosexual put it to Jess Stearn,[26] "Someday we'll outnumber you and you'll be the abnormal ones, and we'll be the normal," there is no real statistical basis for the belief that homosexuality is rapidly increasing. To put it objectively, the biological facts of reproduction make the threat quoted above ridiculous. Homosexuality has always been a social problem, and the marked increase in publicity given it today is only in contrast to, and to some extent the result of, the distorted public and legal attitude toward it in recent generations. Kinsey found:

Frequencies in the homosexual show, on the whole, very little change in older age groups of the two generations. . . . In the youngest adolescent period there seems to be definite increase in frequencies for the younger groups, but after 16 or 20 years of age there are no constant changes. . . . There is, at best, only a slight substantiation for the oft-repeated assertion that "sexual perversion" is on the increase. . . . It is possible that the freer discussion of the homosexual today, both in technical and in popular print, has made the public more conscious of sexual activity that has always been a part of the pattern of the human animal.[27]

There is equally little justification for the assumption that there is a direct correlation between homosexuality and intellectual or artistic ability. It may be simply that the naturally precocious are attracted by homosexual activity because of its nonconformity.[28] Lists of homosexuals who have made outstanding contributions to human culture, such as those mentioned above, can readily be countered with the names of many who have been disastrous in their influence—notably several of the more notorious kings of England.[29] The fact that Broadway and Hollywood are reportedly centers of homosexual activity may be just as readily explained by the hypothesis that the ethos of the theater and the cinema is more receptive of eccentricity and abnormality than by the theory that homosexuals are intrinsically a more sensitive genre. Against the spurious attraction of membership in a fraternity of aesthetes should be put the honest statement of members of the Mattachine Society, an organization devoted to the task of acquiring full civil and social rights for homosexuals: "We are definitely not after recruits," they explained to Jess Stearn. "On the contrary, on the basis of our own experience—the embarrassment, shame and humiliation so many of us have known—we would definitely advise anybody who has not yet become an active homosexual, but has only misgivings about himself, to go the other way if he can." [30]

Many of the difficulties of the homosexual's life are the result of his rejection by society. Some suffer agonies of remorse and self-torture over what they feel to be their immoral desires; whether this arises from conscious identification with the condemnation of church or society, or from neurotic conflict, it can effectively paralyze all initiative and result in a feeling of inferiority which makes social adjustment impossible. Homosexuals are notoriously open to blackmail and other types of intimidation; and because any confession of the acts upon which the pressure is based leads to prosecution, they feel themselves to be outside the normal protection of the law. The ultimate loneliness which the individual homosexual fears is perhaps the expression of the loneliness of a group to whom the normal structures of society—marriage, children, dependents—are closed. John Rechy depicts the terror of the isolated older homosexual:

There is also the panic that one day youll wake up to the fact that youre through on the streets, in the bars—that everyone has had you, that those who havent have lost Interest—that youve been replaced by the fresher faces that come daily into the city in that shifting wave of vagrants—younger than you now (and Youth is at a premium), and now the interest you once felt is focused on someone else. One day someone will say about you: "I had him when he was young and pretty." [31]

Much of this unhappiness could, and should, be eliminated if our society treated homosexuals with normal human decency. But there remains a basic distortion at the core of the homosexual's life which no degree of social integration could correct. Although it may be true that the basic sexual urge is in itself neither heterosexual nor homosexual, but is developed in one direction or the other by social conditioning and experience, it is also true that, to put it mildly, men and women are physically, if not psychologically, made to complement each other. I have argued that procreation cannot be regarded as the *only* natural function of sex; but if there is any facet of sexuality which is natural or normal it is, surely, the capacity to maintain the existence of the race.[32] Since the homosexual's sex life is divorced from one of the basic natural expressions of sex—vaginal coitus—it is always incomplete and always to some extent distorted. Because the natural complementariness of womanhood is rejected, and the fulfilling bond of parenthood impossible, the homosexual's appetite can never be satisfied; he is always searching for "an ideal lover who exists nowhere on the face of this planet." [33]

One symptom of this unfulfilled desire is the fact that male homosexuals are vastly more promiscuous in their sexual contacts than even the more irresponsible heterosexuals. Because for most of them sexual gratification is purely a physical relief and the other man holds no prospect of being a true partner, far more of their encounters approximate to the level of prostitution in the heterosexual's experience. The characteristic male homosexual encounter is a "one-night stand," involving "sex without obligation or commitment." [34] As Donald Cory very frankly admits: "It may be that the homosexual is more in contact with the genitals of the partners, rather than with the whole body and the whole person, than is the heterosexual. For psychological and cultural reasons, it is possible that many homosexuals are having a genital-to-genital relationship, rather than a person-to-person relationship." [35]

Even when two male homosexuals establish a "marriage," the permanence of their never-consummated sexual union is always threatened by disruptive factors additional even to those experienced by normally married people. Both parties to the contract immediately become the object of jealous younger suitors to whom they are easily attracted; and lacking any binding obligation, the relationship has no protection from dissolution. Furthermore, as Anthony Storr points out, the male couple are often more competitive with each other than a man and wife, and "since each generally has an inner sense of inferiority as a man, each will be touchier, more liable to take offense and more inclined to be competitive." [36] Since neither can really satisfy the other, they soon seek another alliance, "sustained by an infinite capacity for blaming each failure on the imperfections and flaws in the partner." [37]

Again, because his sexual desires are never really met, they tend to occupy a disproportionate place in the life and thought of the active homosexual. His social and intellectual pursuits tend to become oriented around, and subordinate to, sexual pursuit. Failing to discover sexual union in which the physical act expresses and embodies a wider and richer bond of love, he is not free to engage in social intercourse uncolored by the unending search for the nonexistent perfect partner. "Homosexuals," writes D. J. West, "get more and more taken up with homosexual groups, adopting the current slang and attitudes, until eventually, except for formal relationships, at work, they have little real contact with the normal world." [38]

Whatever may be the initial attractions of a life which offers independence, nonconformity, varied friendship, and uncomplicated sexual relations, the man who chooses to cultivate his homosexual leanings is entering a fool's paradise. Jess Stearn's comment, at the conclusion of a thorough personal study, that he had yet to meet a truly happy homosexual is worth pondering.[39] So is John Rechy's description of a series of photographs of homosexuals "all staring at the world with a look strangely in common: a look which at first I thought was a coldness behind the smile and then realized must be a kind of muted despair, a franticness to get what the world had offered others and not extended readily to them. . . ." [40]

Of course, most accounts of homosexual life are based upon experiences with those who comprise the clientele of gay bars and engage in overt sexual activity. It must also be remembered that psychiatrists derive their impressions and their facts from men who are in urgent need of therapy. But there are undoubtedly thousands of other men whose homosexual drives are relatively subdued and who would not, even if they were heterosexual, find marriage desirable or necessary. There are many others who have been able, without inner conflict or unhealthy repression, to control their sexual urges except, perhaps, for the outlet of masturbation. D. J. West remarks: "The task becomes less difficult if the individual is fortified by a strong sense of purpose behind his sacrifice, as in the case of a priest, or if he can immerse himself in some cause or activity that will use up the energy he would otherwise expend on the pursuit of love." [41] Nevertheless, the average man with sexual drives of normal strength, who chooses to accept the homosexual role, will probably seek physical satisfaction through contacts with other men and is destined to increasing frustration and ultimate loneliness.

But the question will arise whether the individual has any real choice in the matter. Is it not true, as many people, including most homosexuals believe, that one's sexual orientation is determined by factors beyond control? Has the student with homosexual leanings any freedom to choose whether he will accept that way of life or not? The answer is that he has. There is a large proportion of the campus population that is never likely, so long as there are girls around, to find men at all sexually attractive. There is a very small percentage whose background and experience have, by later adolescence, so affected their make-up as to render any simple choice against homosexuality impossible—though they are unlikely to be beyond professional help. But there is a considerable body of students who have engaged in some homosexual acts since adolescence and found them pleasurable, but who are quite capable, given the knowledge and the opportunity, of developing naturally into normal heterosexuals.

Not a few men are forced into the homosexual milieu because they are discovered in some homosexual activity or relationship and are then assumed quite wrongly by themselves, their peers, and their parents to be "perverts." Rejected by the heterosexual group, ashamed of themselves, and fearful of the law, many such men find acceptance, sympathy, and apparent security among homosexuals. They then become accustomed to homosexual experiences, organize their social lives and even their work around homosexual associations, and eventually find it quite impossible to break free, even if they want to. A knowledge of the facts may well save a student from being forced into, or merely accepting, a condition and a pattern of life he can well escape.

The Unimportance of Early Adult Experience

My second proposition is therefore of great importance: *A large number of men who are not fundamentally or even ex-*

ceptionally homosexual in their orientation have adult homosexual experiences.

Kinsey argued that the tendency to label an individual "homosexual" if he is known to have had a single experience with another individual of the same sex is unfortunate in that it fails to distinguish between the man with a continuous record of unacceptable experiences and the occasional lapse of a man who is otherwise a good father and husband.[42] He pointed out that according to the figures obtained:

> The judge who is considering the case of the male who has been arrested for homosexual activity, should keep in mind that nearly 40 percent of all the other males in the town could be arrested at some time in their lives for similar activity, and that 20 to 30 percent of the unmarried males in that town could have been arrested for homosexual activity that had taken place within that same year.[43]

This did not mean that Kinsey regarded this large proportion as true homosexuals; he argued rather that we should avoid using the terms "homosexual" and "heterosexual" as nouns and speak only of individuals with varying amounts of homo- or heterosexual experience.[44] He found that in his sample, 37 per cent of white males admitted to some homosexual arousal to orgasm after adolescence, although only 4 per cent were exclusively homosexual throughout their lives.[45] The latter figure has been challenged, notably by Edmund Bergler, on the ground that Kinsey's sample was infiltrated by homosexuals wishing to give the impression that they are more numerous than they actually are.[46] However, Kinsey's sample was large and carefully checked, and other authorities tend to confirm that exclusive homosexuals represent from 4 to 5 per cent of the adult male population.[47]

The importance of the figures for our present discussion, however, lies in the demonstration that large numbers of men who have adult homosexual experiences develop normal heterosexual lives. A brief summary of Kinsey's figures for the upper educational group of those who go, or will go, to college makes this even clearer. About one out of every two such men has homosexual experiences in preadolescence; about one out of every five has homosexual experiences between adolescence and fifteen years of age; about one out of every six has such experiences between sixteen and twenty; but only *one out of every twenty among those still unmarried at twenty-five* is exclusively homosexual.[48]

When it is recognized that the latter figure is based on a much smaller number of cases, since the majority marry before twenty-five, it is obvious that there is no necessary connection whatsoever between overt homosexual experience in early adulthood and permanent homosexuality. F. W. Finger, in 1947, found that 27 per cent of a group of students in advanced psychology who replied to a questionnaire admitted at least one adult homosexual episode leading to orgasm, although there was no reason to suppose that the percentage of exclusive homosexuals in the sample was higher than average.[49] Even more striking is the evidence of the group of male students studied by the Kronhausens. They found that although "pseudohomosexual panic" was characteristic of many of these men, "Actually only one or two of them (out of a group of more than 200) showed psychic reactions which were primarily homosexual, and only one of them reported exclusive homosexual relations and no heterosexual outlets during his lifetime." [50] The conclusion is that the man who thinks he has homosexual tendencies should obtain counsel and advice from some competent source, but he should certainly not allow himself to be forced by fear, public pressure, or enticement into adopting the homosexual role.

The Possibility of Change

Furthermore, even if it should appear on examination that the student has markedly homosexual tendencies, *no one within the normal student age range has reason to conclude that his homosexual urges, however strong, are either basic or perma-*

nent. Both the causes of homosexuality and the prospects for cure or alleviation in long-standing cases remain matters of continuing and controversial study among the experts. Indeed, authorities working in this field rival even the most dogmatic theologians in their readiness to excommunicate each other! At the risk of almost certain challenge from some quarter, however, it can be confidently stated that the prospects for cure are good if a man is under twenty-five and desires to lead a heterosexual life. Havelock Ellis wrote:

> A refined and intellectual youth with aesthetic tastes, at the university, for instance, surrounded by attractive and congenial persons of his own sex, may remain indifferent to women and continue to cherish ardent sentimental friendships and admirations, reaching the conclusion that he must be an invert by nature. Yet, when he leaves the university for the world, he discovers that, after all, he shares the common passions of ordinary humanity. It is not, indeed, until the age of twenty-five has been reached or even later, that we can be fairly sure that homosexual impulses are not a phase of normal development.[51]

More recently Dr. D. Curran has emphasized that it is unsafe to diagnose a state of established homosexuality before the age of twenty-five. D. J. West, who quotes him and is, like most British authorities, less optimistic about the prospects for psychiatric cure in later life than many American practitioners, confirms that "many young men who practice homosexuality in their late teens or early twenties grow out of the habit after meeting a suitable woman and settle down to heterosexual life. . . . When homosexual behaviour represents a precarious solution of current conflicts, or reflects the pressure of external circumstances, a change may well come about." [52]

Without entering into the controversial details, we can make a few important statements about the nature of homosexuality in the light of modern knowledge. It is clear, for example, that there is no typical physical type, and the man who is slight or even girlish in build is no more necessarily a homosexual than a burly sailor or a heavyweight boxer, though in an indirect way this effeminacy may contribute to his sexual development. The theory, strongly argued a few decades ago, and still attractive to many confirmed homosexuals who want to avoid any sense of responsibility for continuing their practices, that hereditary, biological, or glandular factors determine the individual's sexual constitution, is now generally abandoned.[53] It is possible that some inherited characteristics may render a man susceptible to homosexual deviation; but without the contributing influences of inadequate family relationships and cultural pressures, these potentialities do not become decisive. Most authorities attribute the homosexual condition to a combination of psychological and sociological factors which prevent the individual from achieving full and free personal relationships with the other sex. A possessive mother, a remote and unresponsive father, an early indoctrination with excessively negative ideas about sex, an unsatisfying or repulsive initial experience with girls, enforced isolation from women, or a combination of these and other circumstances may be to blame. There is no single agreed upon explanation of the dynamics involved, but, in brief, as D. J. West puts it, "Homosexual adaptation occurs when heterosexual adaptation proves too difficult." [54] The condition is the result of "hidden but incapacitating fears of the opposite sex." [55]

This is not the place to enter upon a discussion of the various theories of homosexuality. Whether it is a neurosis, a psychosis, or a symptom of sexual immaturity; whether it is a disease or a way of life; whether the exclusive homosexual is quantitatively or qualitatively different from the man whose normal interests are heterosexual—these remain open questions among the experts. But all are agreed that once firmly implanted, homosexuality is never easy to correct, and is often intractable. Recent studies in the United States suggest that about one-fifth of those established homosexuals *who seek treatment* may achieve a reversal of sexual orientation.[56] Moral exhortations to self-control or heroic ventures into marriage are equally worthless. Psychiatric treatment is painful, expensive, and often unsuccessful. Prevention in this case is worth the fraction of an ounce of cure. Ultimately, the solution depends upon an open and honest attitude toward sex in the family and in society and upon transformed relationships among people. But the most urgent need, and the most hopeful method of attack on the problem, is the dissemination to students faced with this dilemma of the facts contained in this chapter. If ignorance, superstition, and prejudice about homosexuality can be reduced, many can be helped to enjoy full and worth-while heterosexual relationships who might otherwise have been condemned to the unhappiness and emptiness of sex—all male.

9 THE GIRL'S POINT OF VIEW

Men recounting their sexual triumphs very frequently justify overriding the girl's protests by saying something to the effect: "She asked me to stop, but I knew she didn't mean it." This piece of elementary, but inadequate, psychology has its roots in two largely incorrect assumptions. In the first place, there is the unexamined androcentrism of the presumption that most girls find the erotic attentions of a man—particularly the man in question—attractive. In the second place, there is the dangerous half-knowledge, derived from the popular reading of the Kinsey reports, that despite the persistence of Victorian inhibitions about admitting it, women are as sexually responsive as men. The muffled, "Please don't," is taken, quite sincerely, as a mere concession to past convention; the girl is believed to be as fired up as the boy, though she feels it necessary to pretend otherwise. Probably, very few college students would feel happy (unless they were drunk, which is a relevant consideration) about achieving sexual intimacy with a girl they really thought unresponsive or unready for the act. Hence, the necessity for a rationalization of the girl's hesitancy and the assurance with which the all-knowing male interprets her innermost feelings.

Obviously, anyone who sets out to write a chapter on this subject is open to the same attack. What follows is merely the hesitant attempt of one man to communicate to other men what he believes to be the very real differences between male sexuality and that of women. And we can begin with Kinsey, who himself obtained data from nearly 8,000 women as the basis for his volume *Sexual Behavior in the Human Female.*

A Fundamental Difference

Kinsey did conclude that females "appear to be as capable as males of being aroused by tactile stimuli; they appear as capable as males of responding to the point of orgasm." [1] He noted that the average woman responds more slowly than the average man in coitus, but attributed this difference to "the ineffectiveness of the usual coital techniques." [2] He argued that the difference in size between the male penis and the female clitoris has led to the quite mistaken assumption that the quality of erotic pleasure is less in women and that female orgasm is in itself less satisfying than the male.[3] But Kinsey himself went on to attach two riders, which are commonly ignored, to this conclusion; and, in addition, it is becoming clear that his own assessment of female sexuality was distorted by the introduction into the discussion of hidden male criteria.

We noted earlier that Kinsey had brought to light the important fact that men reach the peak of their sexual energy and capacity in the late teens and not, as was previously supposed, in the late twenties.[4] But this statement applies strictly to men only. Women, according to Kinsey, have no particular upsurge in genital arousal at adolescence, and only reach the peak of physical sexual capacity in the middle twenties or even in the early thirties.[5] There is, therefore, absolutely no reason for the young man to assume that because *he* wants to pet to orgasm or engage in intercourse, his girl—even if she is madly in love with him—is either interested in or attracted by the prospect.

The second qualification noted by Kinsey is the fact that women are far less aroused by psychological stimuli to sexual excitement than men are. The average male is readily excited by the thought of coitus; and as soon as a relationship becomes at all intimate, he tends to think in these terms, thus compounding the pressure toward sexual fulfillment. But the average girl, certainly if she is sexually inexperienced, is likely neither to engage in fantasies of coitus nor to be stimulated erotically by such thoughts.[6] Kinsey made a careful and interesting study of thirty-three kinds of erotic psychological stimulation by which the majority of men are affected. These included nude pictures, the genitalia of the other sex, burlesque and floor shows, animals and humans in coitus, erotic stories, lavatory drawings, and discussions about sex.[7] He discovered that the majority of women were largely uninterested in and unaroused by such things. The only two items that produced comparable interest among women were motion pictures (not specifically pornographic) and "literary materials" (i.e., novels, essays, and poetry). And in both these instances, as Kinsey noted, it may well be the romantic element, rather than the explicitly sexual content, which appeals to the woman.[8] But in any case it is obvious that factors leading to intense sexual stimulation in the man may leave his partner cold.

In Kinsey's analysis of the female sex pattern, however, there seems to be a hidden agenda which leads him into some inconsistencies and prevents him from developing the most important point of all. He tends to identify *sexual* arousal with *genital* arousal. If one starts from the strictly biological concern with orgasm as the criterion of sexual experience, as Kinsey did, one necessarily measures female sexual capacity by that criterion as one does the male. But Kinsey does, in fact, go far beyond the purely objective in his discussion of sexual differentia; and here it is impossible to avoid the impression that he has been misled by the unexamined assumption that for women as well as for men, sex is focused in, and primarily fulfilled through, the physical pleasure of genital orgasm. This leads to the entirely gratuitous assumption that women reach *sexual* maturity only in their middle twenties—since they then reach their orgasmic peak, which is (for men) the mark of sexual maturity. Kinsey noted that "as far as physical development is concerned, the girl begins to 'mature' at an earlier age, and *reaches complete maturity before the average boy";* [9] but because he is stuck with the sex-genital identification, he then continues: "While these physical changes at adolescence are a fundamental part of the process by which the female becomes mature enough to reproduce, they seem to have little relation to the development of sexual responsiveness in the female." [10]

The possibility, of which many authorities are now persuaded, that the whole reproductive process initiated by the onset of menstruation is the female equivalent of the male's genital sexual urge was closed to Kinsey. But after all, even in our society with its delayed pattern of marriage, many girls still pass through the years of greatest emotional and psychic intensity *and* bear their first children *before* they ever enjoy the physical pleasure of orgasm. In fact, what appears to the man to be the *ne plus ultra* of burgeoning virility is only the pleasant extra of established relationships and settled family life for many women. This difference is confirmed by the fact that the orgasmic needs of women (which Kinsey confused with their sexual needs) are far more variable than those of men.[11] Moreover, although 96 per cent of women eventually achieve orgasm in marital coitus, this accumulative incidence is not reached until somewhere between thirty-one and forty.[12] And in many cases, orgasm is not frequent at any age.

Ernest Havemann has well summed up the problem that these facts raise for the relationship between the sexes: "To the average woman the average man must indeed seem—simply by virtue of his own physique and glandular system and through no fault of his own—like a 'prancing, leering goat.' To the average man the average woman must seem—simply by virtue of her own physiology and through no coyness or stubbornness of her own—disinterested, unresponsive, and in fact sometimes downright frigid." [13] Basing his conclusions on the researches of Dr. William H. Masters and Mrs. Virginia E. Johnson, he writes:

> The real truth about female sexuality is that it is just as strong as male sexuality and perhaps even stronger; it has seemed weak only because most of its students, being men, have judged it by masculine standards instead of from the woman's point of view. A healthy woman is vitally and intimately concerned with sex from the time she first begins to menstruate, and every new menstrual cycle, calling attention inescapably to the pelvic region, accompanied by strong emotions of elation, depression, eagerness or withdrawal, reaffirms her status as an eminently sexual being. Sex to a man may mean orgasm, but to a woman it means something quite different and even more important.[14]

Psychologists recognize that sexual intercourse is often sought as a means of demonstrating masculinity. A man feels that his manhood is in question and goes out to prove it by overt and often demeaning activity. Women, on the other hand, find their sexuality thrust upon them, as it were, in the inevitable physical and emotional changes of adolescence. A Cambridge college dean caused a considerable stir in England recently by affirming, in a book to which many leading theologians contributed, that premarital intercourse might in some circumstances be not only justifiable but a healing action in which Christ is present.[15] He suggested that a girl might, out of love and concern for another person, give herself to a man in order to help him prove his manhood. He gave as one example the action of the Greek prostitute who, in the movie *Never on Sunday,* gently helps an anxious sailor to achieve confidence and self-respect. Another dramatic illustration would be the action of the schoolmaster's wife who, in *Tea and Sympathy,* reassures a student of his heterosexuality by going to bed with him. Whether such situations occur in real life I do not know. But it is interesting that the examples that come to mind in literature are of women ministering to men. Writing for a male readership, I can confidently affirm that it will not be necessary for any man to engage in intercourse in order to help a woman prove her femininity. Anxiety about one's sexuality is apparently a male obsession. Anthony Storr suggests that the female feels no similar need of reassurance for three reasons: First, she is relatively passive in the sexual act. Second, she does not have to assert the same independence and distinction from the mother as the male. Third, "as Margaret Mead maintains, there is no male equivalent to child bearing, which, in the female, is the source of a deep and sustaining sense of success in the feminine role." [16]

Men like to quote Byron to the effect that "man's love is of man's life a thing apart; 'tis woman's whole existence"; but the apparent implication of male superiority rests upon the failure to understand that love means something very different to a woman. Dorothy Sayers pointed out:

Lovers, husbands, children, households—these are major feminine preoccupations; but not love. It is the male who looks upon amorous adventure as an end in itself, and dignifies it with a metaphysic. The great love-lyrics, the great love-tragedies, the romantic agony, the religion of beauty, the cult of the *ewig Weibliches,* the entire mystique of sex is, in historic fact, of masculine invention.[17]

We must distinguish between the (sometimes exclusively) erotic love which often motivates the male desire for women and the more outgoing, self-giving love which more often characterizes those we so wrongly call (since Pliny) the *sexus infirmus.* Of course, any woman's love, like any man's, contains an element of self-seeking; but the satisfaction she desires is far less likely to be selfish, ephemeral, and physical. She loves a man not for what she can get out of him immediately, but for what she can share with him and give to him. His physique and vigor are important, but they are far less important than the corresponding physical attractions he sees in her. She has far greater interest in the establishment of a permanent relationship which can unite them, and of which physical sexual union is to be an expression and not the essence. Gael Greene concluded that although many a girl in this "orgasm-oriented decade" talks loudly about "the unquenchable fire of her female hormones," her real search is for affection and love.[18]

She Wants Love: He Wants Sex

This profound difference between the man's interest and goal in sexual relations and that of many girls produces highly complex misunderstandings. Because physical intimacy, particularly orgasm, is less central to the girl's sexual development, the partners in a dating process can easily be at odds without understanding why. "Both sexes," writes Gael Greene, "promise more than they deliver and demand more than the original contract specified. 'He only wants sex,' the coed may say. 'She doesn't give a damn about me,' the boy replies, 'only wants to know where I'm planning to take her.' "[19] For the man, advanced petting or intercourse is likely to be desirable, whether his feeling for the girl is deep or not. For her it is more likely to be unattractive or even repugnant if no romantic relationship exists. If she finds the man attractive and enjoys his company, the girl will accept further intimacies, not because she desires them but because he does and she wants to please him. She may assume, quite wrongly, that since (for her) passionate love-making would be the expression of a deep commitment, the boy's persistence and enthusiasm reflect a similar commitment. He, for his part, may equally, wrongly suppose that her readiness for petting reflects (as it would in him) erotic passion, and then may place her under pressure to go further than she really wishes. It is only later, and perhaps too late, that she realizes that what had been for her a peripheral concession, an expression of regard or of appreciation, he had interpreted as an invitation to full venereal satisfaction. What seems to the man an obvious and extremely desirable conclusion to an evening together, worth all the possible risks (mostly to the girl), may be to her an entirely superfluous and even unattractive proceeding to which she only agrees because she loves him. As Dr. Mary Calderone has written: "The girl plays at sex, for which she is not ready, because fundamentally what she wants is love; and the boy plays at love, for which he is not ready, because what he wants is sex." [20]

Because her total physical and psychic being reaches maturity earlier than the boy's, the girl is often the more sophisticated socially and the better able to direct a relationship in the initial stages. Because of her orientation toward the permanent fulfillment of sexuality in marriage and childbearing, she is far less interested in casual intimacies than the man. Even Helen Gurley Brown recognized that what the single girl really wants to hear is not, "You're beautiful, you're sexy, you're the love of my life," but simply, "Will you marry me?" [21] Kinsey found that nine out of ten women indicated some moral (though not necessarily religious) objection to premarital intercourse, whereas hardly more than half that number of men felt any qualms about it.[22]

A correspondent in the London *Observer,* a few years ago, was surely right when he pointed out, "It is mistaken to suppose that most affairs are indulged in fearlessly by a man and a woman with their eyes wide open and their consciences clear. More usually the situation derives from persistent importuning by the man, and eventual surrender by the girl, who is either frightened of losing her man, or too tired to resist."

I am not saying that girls are uninterested in sex or in men, nor that coeds never really enjoy the physical experience of coitus and orgasm. I am not suggesting that all women are paragons of retiring virtue, anxiously preserving their virginity until "Mr. Right" comes along. On the contrary, there are plenty of teenagers who are aggressively ready to "lose it." Nor am I arguing that the present situation is unalterable. It may be that when fear of pregnancy is finally eliminated by the availability of a safe and simple contraceptive, the girl's reluctance to engage in intercourse will vanish away. Personally, I doubt it, as do many authorities, and it is interesting to note that Kinsey believed that the differences in sexual responsiveness between males and females depended on differences in nervous organization.[23] But we are dealing with the present, and all the evidence available goes to show that the average responsible girl regards sex without love and affection as a bore and a waste.[24] Indeed, even the most promiscuous and aggressively-pleasure-seeking girl is frequently using her physical equipment (almost always unsuccessfully) as a means to achieving acceptance and affection. From Kirkendall's study, it becomes clear that at every level of liaison, from the casual pick-up to the formal engagement, girls tend to see the sexual encounter in terms of a permanent relationship and eventual marriage.[25]

Nor am I saying that nice girls don't go to bed with importunate boys. The fact is that many of them do, though they would prefer not to, because of overwhelming pressures. Our culture still places most girls in the position of eventual dependence on a man for the necessities of life—quite apart from his contribution in procreation—and the fear of being excluded from marriage because of unrealistic standards of morality is extremely strong. Moreover, in addition to the persistent pressure of the men in her life, the coed has to cope with the social impact of campus expectations. Mary S. Calderone has spoken of her surprise at discovering that women freshmen, although able and ready to deal with the demands of their dates, could not withstand the demands of their own upperclassmen that they conform to campus mores by having sexual intercourse.[26] Max Lerner has given a vivid picture of the tensions faced by the contemporary coed:

> She is riddled with anxieties, determined to belong, fearful of being left behind—by the boys, by the rival girls, by fun, by popularity, by experience, by marriage, by life. She plays it cool, yet is boastful of her sexual drive and hedonism. She has discarded the traditional moral absolutes, living in a world of relativism that at once frees her from the old restraints, yet leaves her pathetically floundering with little sense of limits. When she tries to apply "wait until marriage" as her frame of limits, the boys mock her and she panics at the fear of being outdistanced in the competition. When she tries to apply the "everything but—" standard, either through parental teaching or through fear of pregnancy, she is cursed as a teaser or ends in a tangle of contradictions, missing expressiveness and morality at once.[27]

The girl's dilemma is beautifully dramatized in the sketch by *The Committee,* to which reference was made earlier.[28] Si, trying to persuade Sharon to go to bed with him, points out that they have been going together for a long time, sharing many things. "Now we've come to a point in our relationship where we can share something far greater, much more important, much more beautiful," he pleads. But Sharon replies, "Look, Si. I can't just do it for a sharing experience. What if I did share with you, and then I found out I didn't love you. So then I met somebody else and had deep feelings for them too, and so then I shared with them. . . . And then I met somebody else and I just kept on sharing and sharing and sharing."

Mutual understanding between the sexes is further complicated by the fact that in many instances the girl wants the man to want intercourse—but she equally wants him to desist when she asks him to. As one English teenager put it, "You're annoyed if a boy tries to make you on the first date because it shows he thinks you're easy, and you're annoyed if he *doesn't* try to make you because it shows he doesn't fancy you." [29] It is not surprising that boys, lacking any profound insight into female psychology and sexuality, find this attitude irrational. Equally perplexing to the male is the fact that once the relationship has reached a certain degree of depth and permanence, the girl may be quite prepared to agree to intercourse when she has previously resisted this step. But this is not nearly so surprising if we remember that the sex act in itself may be quite unimportant to the girl in her teens or early twenties. Yet what holds no appeal for her at all as a casual physical experience in the context of purely superficial relationship, she may be quite ready to give (because it seems to mean so much to the boy she now loves) once the relationship is established on a sound basis.

This apparent ambivalence, though actually quite consistent from the girl's point of view, poses serious threats to the relationship. For the girl it means that at this point she may well get badly hurt. If the man is less than absolutely honest with her and with himself, he can very easily lead her into actions which she will bitterly regret. Boys are often able to sense the needs of a girl for certain characteristics and then to mislead her into thinking that he embodies her ideal. If she has begun to feel deeply for him and believes the relationship to hold promise of permanence, she may be ready to accept intercourse in the hope that he shares her commitment. But if it turns out later that he has misled her, perhaps quite unintentionally, and that she has given herself without mutual love, then self-disgust, shame, and suffering may result.

The Kronhausens report the following perceptive account of such an experience:

I met a girl and started making love to her. Eventually she fell in love with me. (At least she thought she loved me and that, I think, amounts to the same thing. In other words, she could be badly hurt.) One day we were alone in my father's home and we decided to make love. This we accomplished in a bedroom on the second floor. After we finished, she wanted to be kissed and to hear that I loved her—anything at all that would *justify the act*. What she did not know was that *I felt nothing but a physical attraction for her* and wanted no part of her after we were finished. . . . For the first time I realized the damage I had done.[30]

What to the man may be just another sexual adventure may be in the thought of the girl the beginning of a relationship leading to marriage. When he assures her in the moment of passion, "I love you," he may mean only, "I want you," but she may assume that the words have the same meaning for him as they do for her. An experience which he can shrug off without embarrassment or guilt may be to her the source of long-lasting pain and anguish. The number of girls who later regret their sexual experience is not as high as some moralists have claimed, but Kinsey found that one girl in three of those who had engaged in premarital intercourse had some regrets.[31] Allowing for the healing influence of time and the fact that nearly half the girls had only engaged in coitus with the men they later married, this suggests that a large proportion of those girls who are involved in casual affairs suffer permanent hurt. Whether he likes it or not, the man has the responsibility, once a relationship becomes at all serious, of deciding how far to arouse the response and expectations of the girl.

Mary S. Calderone has suggested that the following question should be addressed to every young male:

Before you make love to a girl, you have an obligation to come to a deliberate decision in full awareness that you will be setting in motion powerful forces in that girl. If you are concerned about her as a human being, you must decide whether or not it is appropriate at her age and stage of development to learn sexual response. And you must decide whether she is ready for this. If you think she is, then you should acknowledge that it will certainly affect her life to some degree, and perhaps more profoundly than you can imagine.[32]

Dr. Calderone would underline the fact that the woman is *vulnerable* in the sexual relationship in a way that the man is not—not merely because she may become pregnant, but because sex means something deeper and more significant to her.

But it is also possible for the boy, through ignorance, to be needlessly hurt, and perhaps to break up a relationship which is potentially healthy. Many a young man still adopts the double standard, according to which, although he is free to seek coitus from every available girl, he has the right to expect that any girl upon whom he bestows the privilege of marriage should be a virgin. If he is seriously interested in a girl as a marriage partner, he therefore takes it for granted that she will resist his desires right up to the wedding night. Not infrequently, he may test her by suggesting intercourse, even though he does not want her to agree to it. If she yields to his blandishments, he may conclude that she has let him down and is nothing but a tramp. Alternately, having depended largely upon her greater maturity and restraint to maintain the limits of intimacy, he may be thrown off kilter by the sudden change in power and give way to impulses which he will regret more than she. Frequently, a man affirms that he has "lost respect" for a girl following intercourse, when this is only a rationalization of his own sense of guilt.[33] Or he may succumb to the false suspicion that she is using intercourse as a means of trapping him into marriage. There are indeed girls of whom Gael Greene says that they are quite prepared to use their biological potential as another weapon in the arsenal of the husband hunt.[34] But in the great majority of cases, nothing so calculating as cold-blooded blackmail is involved. It is simply that the girl hopes intercourse will please the boy, for whom she has a real affection, and place the relationship on a more permanent basis. Whether the man should, for the sake of both of them, take advantage of her readiness, we shall consider in the next chapter. The possibility must be weighed that he should conclude, "Because I love her, I won't."

10 LOVE MAKES IT RIGHT

The crux of the sexual dilemma, for most students, was succinctly formulated as long ago as 1721 in a debate held that year at Harvard: "Whether it be Fornication to lye with one's Sweetheart before Marriage." Any responsible man is likely, whatever his actual practice may be, to acknowledge to himself that sexual satisfaction divorced from affection and respect for the other person is debased and unnatural in a human being. The use of a prostitute to satisfy mere curiosity or for the release of sexual tension is frequently reported, even among the small number of contemporary students who resort to it, to be unsatisfying, revolting, or humiliating.[1]

Again, few men of maturity are happy with themselves if they achieve a "quick lay" with a casual date, however easily they may be carried away by urgent desire. Lester A. Kirkendall, in a study of two hundred college-level men with sexual experience, found that only a small percentage of those who had engaged in this type of liaison declared themselves satisfied with the exploitive use of a girl for physical pleasure or the demonstration of masculine prowess.[2] Most men of integrity who are aware of the harm they may do to a sensitive girl will try to avoid overriding her scruples by placing her under emotional pressure or by taking advantage of her eagerness for a permanent relationship.[3] Yet it is generally taken for granted that such hesitations are irrelevant once a serious mutual attachment has been achieved.

"So long as nobody gets hurt," runs the argument, "love makes it right." The student quoted at some length at the end of Chapter 4 put it most persuasively:

If we deeply love one another, and we find in sex a way of showing its deepest levels; if we find that during and after and because of it we are straining to grow in stature in the other's eyes; if we find that because it is loving, the release of the sex energy also releases, rather than uses up, our deepest creative energies; if each time there is a sexual interlude, we find we love and respect and admire each other more afterwards, then, and only then, but so sensitively and wonderfully then, *it is right.*[4]

Traditional Objections Re-examined

I have already made it clear that I have no sympathy with the traditional religious and social dismissal of all sexual activity outside marriage as immoral, or with the too-simple labeling of all premarital intercourse as "fornication." Many of the intimacies which our society condones or encourages, such as petting, may be more reprehensible when indulged in for purely physical pleasure than intercourse between a boy and a girl deeply in love. Moreover, there is no evidence to support the view that when an engaged couple sleep together, some harm is always necessarily done to their future marriage. Kirkendall found that when intercourse was accepted freely by both parties and on the basis of a long-standing mutual commitment, it sometimes did no damage to the relationship.[5] On the other hand, he also found that in some cases considerable harm resulted, sometimes quite unexpectedly, and any young man who ignores the complexity of the factors involved can hardly settle the dilemma of sex with any confidence of success.

The two chief weapons in the armory of those who would (surely quite immorally) frighten young men and women into chastity are almost entirely ineffective as deterrents today. Nevertheless, the facts cannot be ignored. Kinsey's statement, as recently as 1953, that "present methods of simple and rapid cure for both syphilis and gonorrhea make their spread through premarital coitus a relatively unimportant matter" has proved to be entirely premature.[6] The overoptimistic assumption that penicillin and other drugs would eliminate these twin curses has led to a false sense of security, and at present venereal diseases are rampant in epidemic proportions in thirty major American cities.

Cases of syphilis in persons under twenty years old are estimated to have increased by 200 per cent between 1960 and 1965.[7] And in January, 1964, the chief of the Ohio Health Department's Communicable Diseases Division warned: "More, and more, . . . it is appearing among middle and upper economic class people—business people, professional people. And it used to be almost exclusively a disease that occurred in large cities. It still does, but it is appearing more and more in small communities and rural areas." According to the Surgeon General of the United States, 1,500 young Americans contract venereal disease *every day in the year*.[8] Much of this horrifying increase is due to homosexual activity. It is obviously irrelevant to engaged couples who never have coitus except with each other. But, without again elevating the threat of VD to the status of a decisive deterrent, it is clearly a fact of which every one should take account.

The possibility of pregnancy is also largely ignored in the thinking of most male students, although Gael Greene reported that it is one of the most common factors (though not frequently the decisive factor) quoted when girls analyze what keeps them from accepting intercourse.[9] And the fear is by no means as ill-founded as is commonly supposed. The magical pill has not solved the problem: it is not even generally understood by male students that it has to be used throughout the whole menstrual cycle to be effective. Girls, except those who feel themselves committed to uninhibited promiscuity, neither take the pill as a regular safeguard nor wear a diaphragm for all occasions.[10] The majority take the entirely superstitious view, "It can't happen to me" [11]—and the result is that *one out of every five girls who have intercourse before marriage becomes pregnant*.[12] Despite all the increased knowledge and discussion of birth control, the number of illegitimate births among teenagers doubled between 1940 and 1961, and in the same period the number for the twenty to twenty-five age group nearly quadrupled.[13]

Moreover, it must be remembered that unwanted pregnancies are more likely to occur among those who are least promiscuous.

Those who plan consciously to go all the way normally take the necessary precautions. But many students, of both sexes, who really want to avoid intercourse, fail to plan for the eventuality because such premeditation runs contrary to their best intentions. They are then carried away by high passion after an enjoyable evening together and take a risk which proves disastrous. Even when an attempt at contraception is made, college students are notoriously ill-informed and inefficient. It is also true that the very people who emphasize the romantic element in sexual relationships frequently regard any mechanical contraceptive device as an interference with the spontaneity of the act, or as a debasement. Although they may be the last to yield to the urge to engage in coitus, they are the most likely to reap the consequences in conception.

Of course, the consequences of extramarital pregnancy are by no means as serious as they were even a few decades ago. Yet, once again, it is as stupid to minimize them as it is unconvincing to exaggerate them. Abortion is the most common solution. Despite the fact that it is illegal, it can be readily arranged in the United States, and the report of the Institute for Sex Research makes it clear that neither the cost nor the risk to health is as serious as many imagine.[14] They found that some unfavorable consequences were reported by one-third of the girls interviewed, but in most cases these were minor, and significant psychological effects occurred in less than 10 per cent of the cases.[15] Gael Greene found that although horror stories of abortion were widespread among college girls, "the girls who described their *own* experiences with illegal abortions rarely spoke in terms of horror or strong repulsion." [16] Yet profound psychological trauma, serious physical harm, and occasionally death do result from induced abortions, and it would seem that the man who really loves a girl will hardly take comfort from the statistical fact that she is not *likely* to suffer seriously. The more concerned he is, the less he is likely to be prepared to allow her to undergo an abortion that involves even a slight risk to her life.

The consequence is that the majority of responsible and mature couples who engage in premarital intercourse accept the fact that they are parents of a child and get married. Although this is certainly undesirable if there is no real bond of love and no prior thought of marriage, an early wedding under duress can be the prelude to permanent happiness. The social stigma attached to childbirth within nine months of marriage is relatively slight today, and there is even one State in the Union which will provide an antedated marriage certificate to prevent embarrassment to the baby in later years.

But the possible threats to the success of a marriage occasioned by its beginning under the cloud of necessity are not to be ignored. Instead of the couple having a number of years in which to cement their relationship and prepare for the challenge of children, they start their marriage with the additional demands of parenthood. Consciously or unconsciously, there may be hostility against the child or the partner for interrupting a career. When the inevitable later strains develop, there may be an unexpressed feeling that *if* there had been no baby on the way, one or other would have broken the engagement before marriage. These reactions may often be avoided or overcome, but they are significant possibilities to be weighed against the attractions of premarital intercourse.

The Test of Suitability

Having put the traditional objections in some balanced light, we must now take an equally honest look at the supposed advantages of going to bed unwed. One widely accepted argument is that intercourse is a final necessary test of the suitability of the couple for each other. There is a certain contradiction between this approach and the romantic declaration, "I love her and I'm going to marry her anyway, so why not?" But perhaps nobody uses both arguments at the same time. The question I would put is, "What do you expect to find out about each other through intercourse before marriage that you do not already know, or that you cannot better find out when you are already married and embarked on the discipline of life together?" Let us assume (rather optimistically, perhaps) that a couple know each other in the terms described by one of the students in the Kronhausen study:

I think I do love her; that is, if love means: that you want to see the girl every day, that you enjoy spending time with her, that you always want to do favors for her, that you are able to talk of marriage and can somehow visualize being married to her, that we are happy and satisfied sexually, that we sometimes have arguments which we both admit to having started, that we go out of our way to please each other, that we say that we love each other, and that we have planned marriage.[17]

What more do they need to know, or can they know, that is necessary as a preliminary to marriage? What, given this degree of mutual understanding and honesty between two people, could be a good reason for failing to get married? What, in particular, is intercourse going to prove or disprove?

Well, one possible answer is that they might discover whether one or the other is sterile, and whether they will be able to have children; but quite apart from the fact that several years continuous experimentation would be necessary to prove anything, the experiment is usually conducted in such a way that the primary objective is *not* to become pregnant! In our culture, again, it is hardly necessary to have intercourse to discover whether you arouse some sexual response in each other. From the first sexual encounter—and remember that this begins when you first hold hands—you become aware of mutual erotic stimulation, which is fully tested in necking and petting activities. *Pace* Helen Gurley Brown, very few girls and even fewer boys need to go as far as bed to discover whether the partner is homosexual.[18]

In Mary McCarthy's novel *The Group,* Dottie Renfrew and her mother agreed that an engaged couple ought to have intercourse once to make sure of a happy adjustment, because her mother "knew of some very sad cases within her own circle of friends where the man and the woman just didn't fit down there and ought never to have been married." [19] If the reference is to the man's inability to achieve erection, this is certainly a matter for professional counsel; but it can hardly be unknown to him in the course of heavy petting activities. If the reference is to the purely physical proportions of the male and female sex organs, instances of serious or permanent difficulty are almost unknown. There may be physical factors, such as an unusually tough hymen, which make intercourse temporarily impossible. But suppose a couple attempts intercourse before marriage and are unsuccessful; what are they going to do? Decide that despite their love for each other they are not suited, and break up over a problem which, if discovered after marriage, would almost certainly be cleared up by medical treatment? They may, of course, find that the girl has difficulty reaching orgasm during intercourse; but despite what the marriage handbooks say, this is a common experience which only patient attention—perhaps for several years—will overcome. Opportunities for intercourse before marriage, especially when they are rushed or threatened with interruption (as many still are, despite the convenience of motels), frequently make the necessary relaxation impossible for the girl. To part company then, because they cannot reach a mutual climax after one or two or many attempts may be to break up a wonderful relationship which could have blossomed into perfect sexual accord within marriage. In other words, as a test of suitability premarital intercourse tells us nothing of significance that cannot be discovered in other ways. And what it may appear to tell us is more likely to be misleading than helpful.

Premarital Intercourse and Marriage

A second popular argument in favor of premarital intercourse is to the effect that it makes for better and happier marital relationships. The "Playboy Forum," for example, recently affirmed that, in the Kinsey studies, "a significant correlation was found between premarital sexual experience and successful marriage."[20] But this widespread impression is not justified by the facts, and Kinsey drew no such conclusion. What he did find was that there was a marked correlation between the experience of orgasm in coitus by a girl before marriage and her capacity to reach orgasm in coitus during the early years of marriage.[21] But, whereas there is no doubt that in the long run the achievement of mutual physical satisfaction in coitus is a significant factor in the permanence and success of marriage, there is no reason to suppose that the achievement of orgasm early in marriage is an indicator of a mature marriage relationship. Indeed, in view of Kinsey's own findings that women often do not reach their orgasmic peak until their late twenties, and in view of the recent recognition that this is not, for them, the significant criterion of sexuality that it is for the male, orgasm in early marriage may be largely an irrelevant criterion of success for the woman.[22]

There are many women who do respond earlier to physical sexual arousal, and achieve coital orgasm both before marriage and in the early years of marriage. It may be that the earlier experience of satisfying coitus is the cause of quicker adjustment within marriage, and Kinsey believed this to be the case. But it may also be simply that girls with earlier sexual interests (in the male sense of the term) and fewer inhibitions are more ready to engage in premarital intercourse, and that if they had not done so they would still have responded early in marriage. Kinsey acknowledged this possibility:

> The most responsive females may have been the ones who had had the largest amount of premarital experience and, because they were responsive, they were the ones who had most often reached orgasm in marriage. The females who had abstained before marriage may have been the physiologically less responsive individuals who, therefore, were the ones who had most often remained chaste, both before and after marriage.[23]

But, in either case, evidence is lacking to show that girls of this type, or girls with this experience, make the most successful marriage partners, as distinct from the most enjoyable bed partners on the honeymoon. Hamblin and Blood argued that a more careful analysis of the Kinsey data showed that experience or inexperience in premarital intercourse shows no consistent causal relationship to sexual adjustment in marriage.[24] Burgess and Wallin, in an independent study, *Engagement and Marriage,* concluded that on the whole a husband and wife *without* experience of premarital intercourse have a higher chance of marital success.[25]

Furthermore, Kinsey noted two negative considerations which should make the advocate of premarital intercourse hesitate. In the first place, it is quite clear that unsatisfactory or unsuccessful experience in coitus before marriage is very likely to make sexual adjustment after marriage more difficult for the woman. Kinsey wrote:

> It should be emphasized that premarital coital experience which had not led to orgasm (perhaps because of moral or religious doubts about the practice) had not correlated with successful sexual relations in marriage. On the contrary *it showed a high correlation with failure in the marital coitus.* . . . a girl who becomes involved in premarital coitus in which she does not respond may be traumatically affected by such experience, and thus be handicapped in her later adjustments in marriage.[26]

In the second place, Kinsey found a marked correlation between premarital intercourse and extramarital intercourse. To put it bluntly, the girl who goes to bed before marriage is about twice as likely, according to Kinsey's figures, to go to bed with someone other than her husband after marriage.[27] Once again, whether the premarital intercourse is the cause or the effect cannot be established. But Kinsey recognized that "it is not impossible that nonmarital coital experience before marriage had persuaded those females that nonmarital coitus might be acceptable after marriage." [28] I would not want to put any great weight on this correlation, nor to question that in many cases a couple who have engaged in coitus before marriage remain faithful to each other afterward. But I do want to point out that these various qualifications greatly reduce the value of Kinsey's statistics as *evidence* for the view that premarital intercourse increases the prospects for a full and meaningful relationship in marriage.

On the contrary, there is reason to believe that moving into intercourse has a contrary effect upon engagement and eventual marriage in many instances. Kirkendall found that one-third of the engaged men he interviewed had feelings of guilt or regret following intercourse. Many reported tensions between them and their fiancées, and there was frequently a breakdown in mutual communication and understanding.[29] Of twenty-eight men who had engaged in coitus with fiancées, five had given up intercourse (mostly because they felt it endangered their relationship), and seven had broken the engagement.[30] When we remember that the breaking of an engagement is, especially for the girl, much more difficult after coitus, the latter figure is extremely significant. It indicates that at least one man in four finds that the girl he thought he loved, and with whom he had intercourse on this "moral" basis, proved in fact not to be the girl he eventually married. We can hardly avoid considering the effects of such broken engagements upon the status of the girl who has agreed, or been persuaded, to "lose it" for the man she thought she would marry. Kinsey found that one out of every two upper-level males under twenty-five stated that he intended to marry a virgin, or at least a girl who had only slept with him before marriage.[31] Although this double standard is probably less rigorously applied today, it still has many advocates. "It's okay for me to sleep with your sister, but it's not okay for you to sleep with mine," said a Harvard graduate student recently.[32] This means that the man who persuades his girl to have intercourse, and doesn't eventually marry her, often puts her out of the market for the kind of marriage he thinks most desirable. Of course, he may not love her enough to worry about that prospect; but in that case does he love her enough to justify intercourse on the basis from which this discussion started?

The Religious Objection

At this point we must reconsider the position of those who believe that premarital intercourse is altogether undesirable. I am not thinking of the traditional religious view, which settles the issue simply by appeal to the biblical or ecclesiastical condemnation of fornication. That approach, now that it has little support from the threat of pregnancy or VD, carries weight with few students, in my experience. However, it is worth pointing out that anybody who has serious religious objections to premarital intercourse and allows himself to be seduced or pressured into it by his peers or his emotions is courting trouble. "For a person who believes that premarital intercourse is morally wrong," wrote Kinsey, "there may be, as the specific histories show, conflicts which do damage not only to marital adjustments, but to the entire personality of the individual." [33] And it must be recognized that the possibility that such harm will be done to the girl with deep religious objections is much greater.

There are, however, more rational and convincing arguments, based upon the connection between sex and personal relationships, in favor of preserving the experience of intercourse until marriage. The first of these can be illustrated from that touching and beautiful story, *A Taste of Honey*. In the course of discussion about relations with men, the extremely promiscuous Ellen tells her daughter, Jo, "You always remember the first time"—and it is quite clear from the development of the drama that Jo will indeed remember the first time with a mixture of joy and sorrow. Otto Piper has argued that the first experience of coitus involves a critical discovery of the self and of the other person—of the essence of masculinity and femininity—which should be experienced only with the woman with whom one is to share one's life. "The sexual act leads to a new and deepened understanding of oneself which is characterized by three features: it is an intuitive knowledge given in and with the sexual experience; it discloses what was thus far hidden from the individual;

and its subject matter is one's Self seen in the mutual relationship in which it stands with the partner's Self." [34]

In this view, therefore, to engage in coitus with any girl other than the one the man marries is to deny to her and to himself the privilege of sharing together in a unique experience—an experience which no future act of intercourse can embody. William Hamilton has put the point effectively:

> If it is true that sexual intercourse mediates a unique kind of personal knowledge, it is clear that a very special status must be given to the first experience of the sexual act. While, in a marriage, new things are always being learned about the other by a couple truly in love, it is also true that a decisive importance must be attached to the first time this mutual and intimate knowledge was ever shared. . . . The first sexual experience is so overwhelming and so different from any other experience that it is better reserved as a means of symbolizing and giving meaning to marriage.[35]

Another rather metaphysical approach has been cogently presented by Sherwin Bailey, whose original contributions to this whole subject we have already noted. He suggests that, man being a unity of body and spirit, sexual intercourse is "a personal encounter between man and woman in which each does something to the other for good or for ill, which can never be obliterated." [36] When a couple lie together (other than in cases of rape or the seduction of the young or feeble-minded), he believes that they truly become "one flesh," whether they realize it or not. However much their future actions may deny it, this union, or *henosis,* remains a profoundly significant reality which affects their very being. If they are married, it provides the basis for ever-deepening community between them. If they are not "they merely enact a hollow, ephemeral, diabolical parody of marriage which works disintegration in the personality and leaves behind a deeply seated sense of frustration and dissatisfaction—though this may never be brought to the surface of consciousness and realized." [37] This understanding of the significance of intercourse, like that of Piper, has firm roots in the biblical idea of man's nature and sexuality. Obviously, the man to whom it is convincing, and who wants to enjoy all the richness of personal union, will avoid establishing empty and superficial relationships with women other than the one he marries.

The Final Intimacy and the Final Commitment

Both these approaches, although they avoid any purely dogmatic appeal to authority, are likely to seem highly doctrinaire and idealistic to many readers of this book. I think that two other considerations may be more relevant and persuasive. First, I would ask whether the act of intercourse, with all its unique quality and intimacy, can be rightly or meaningfully experienced apart from the permanent commitment of marriage. Does not love, in any profound sense, remain unfulfilled until the couple are actually responsible for each other? And if so, can the act which expresses and seals the unity of love be justified in advance of that moment? Should the man who has not yet taken the decisive step of committing his future to a girl ask of her this risk to her future? If he does not yet share his economic and domestic life with her, is he ready to share this unity of body with her? There is, after all, a real difference between the relationship of a couple before and after marriage. Before, even in the most sincere and honest engagement, neither is fully and objectively responsible for the other. After the wedding they are legally, socially, and personally committed beyond recall, no longer independent centers of action but "one flesh." Even trial marriage is an entirely different relationship, because in this experiment people are trying each other out, rather than committed to each other. Indeed, a trial marriage is a contradiction of terms, because the essence of marriage is that (at least in intention) it is not a trial at all but a permanent bond. And if the full meaning of sex is discovered in personal relationships, the ultimate intimacy of intercourse should be preserved until the ultimate commitment to another person, which is represented by marriage.

A man who really loves a girl he is dating or engaged to cannot ignore the fact that at the moment she is not his wife, that

she has not yet left father and mother and become one flesh with him. She is still a member of her parental family, not of his. Although he may not feel any special obligation to that family, she does; and although he may be quite ready to act as if they were already married, she may have serious reservations. If he is a responsible human being, he will at least take account of the possibility that in persuading or allowing her to act contrary to the judgment of her family, he may be treating her as a thing rather than as a person—using her and her love in order to satisfy his own urgent need of sexual release.

Second, I think that the radical dissociation of coitus and reproduction involves a distortion of human sexuality. I have already made it clear that I dissent vigorously from the traditional ecclesiastical view that reproduction is the only, or even the primary, justification for sexual intercourse. But I would argue that it is one of the proper and fundamental implications of any true sexual union. I do not mean that it is necessary in every instance, or even in most instances, that procreation must be an open possibility to justify or fulfill sexuality. I do not mean that the childless couple are incapable of a deep and satisfying union: they already have a family in themselves, and their hope for children is frustrated by factors beyond their control. On the other hand, the unmarried couple approach intercourse with an anxious repudiation of the possibility of parenthood. The balance, meaning, and unity of human sexuality is therefore distorted because one of its natural consequences and joys—as well as one of its challenges and costs—is rejected and feared as utterly inappropriate in the circumstances. To enjoy coitus in the safe period, or with the safeguard of contraception, within the context of a married relationship in which the responsibility and privilege of parenthood are accepted (whether or not it has already been achieved) is one thing. To clutch at the immediate pleasure of intercourse while one of its natural ends is absolutely renounced is quite another. Particularly for many girls, the total isolation of intercourse from reproduction involves a kind of sexual anarchy. If the man feels little of this complication, he should at least ask himself whether, for her sake, the argument should run: "I love her—that makes it wrong until we're married." Under the emotion of physical stimulation, it is extremely difficult for a girl to refuse intercourse to a man she loves, and this places a special responsibility on the man, who is more likely to be the advocate of "going all the way." Love surely requires of us that we respect the actual (and not merely the expressed) sensibilities and interests of the other person.

So much can be said not only in defense but in honor of waiting until marriage. But I would wish to avoid elevating a principle and an ideal, however sound, into an absolute law—especially since experience suggests that no absolute and clear-cut application of the principle is possible. In our culture, as we have seen, the young couple are often trapped between the premature arousal of their sexual instincts and economic barriers that society places in the way of early marriage. In the circumstances it is almost inevitable that they will sometimes justifiably anticipate that union which should, ideally and perfectly, be consummated only after the commitment of marriage. If intercourse is accepted mutually after full and free discussion by a couple planning to be married, if there is a clear acceptance of the possibility of pregnancy and a readiness for the sacrifices it will involve, and if they are mature and established in their respect and love for each other, it is quite possible that the act will be little different in its significance for them if it precedes marriage. Certainly, it need not be inconsistent with eventual marital success and happiness. Even those adults who are most ready to cluck their tongues when they hear of a premarital pregnancy, or those clergy who are most prone to inveigh against the sinfulness of anticipating the wedding night can usually, if they examine their own experiences or those of their friends, discover at least one happily married couple who engaged in premarital intercourse.

I have always been impressed by the advice of Canon Bryan Green, of Birmingham, England, who tells students that when an engaged couple who are in love find themselves engaging in intercourse they should thank God for the experience and ask forgiveness for the lack of discipline. This dictum, on at least one occasion, produced in the newspaper of a town where Canon Green was conducting a preaching mission the headline: GREEN GIVES GREEN LIGHT TO SIN. Sin it may be, in technical terms, insofar as it falls short of perfection; but it is at least a very-warm-hearted sin compared with some of the cold sins of pride, exploitation, and indifference to humanity upon which the churches and society have always looked with much greater patience and sympathy.

I would have to go further than this, and say that in some circumstances, intercourse before marriage may be an alternative to something worse—the withering and death of a meaningful and valuable relationship which cannot yet, for completely good reasons, be consummated in marriage. The too-easy assumption by moralists that the act will always be expressive of lust or selfishness is simply not true to the facts. Kirkendall records a number of occasions on which intercourse had definitely enabled a couple to gain in understanding, trust, and love for each other.[38] And what is most striking about these accounts is the fact that far from becoming an obsession and pandering to merely physical desire, coitus, once it had been accepted, fell into proper proportion in relation to the wider interests and mutual comfort of engagement. One example is worth quoting:

We had held strongly all during our courtship to what we regarded as a Christian pattern of sexual conduct, that is, avoidance of premarital intercourse. We had been going together for over a year and were wanting to get married. I was eighteen and my fiancée the same age. My parents were opposed to our marriage, and we were just "spinning our wheels." . . . It was at this point that we went into intercourse. As I look back at it—it was about a year ago that this happened—I think I can see several reasons for what we did. We were so frustrated and blocked that intercourse did two things for us. First, we needed to be close to each other, and this was the way we could get the closeness we wanted. Second, it helped me feel that in spite of the objection of my parents, we were moving toward marriage. Actually, in a certain Christian sense, we were already married after intercourse. Then, perhaps there was an element of spite against our parents in what we did. It is all very complex.[39]

One friend of mine who read the original lectures upon which this book is based remarked: "It won't make any difference whether they go to bed before marriage or not. And why don't you tell them so honestly?" My answer is twofold. First, I do not conceive it to be my responsibility to tell the reader anything so dogmatic and oversimplified. Most students will not determine their conduct by any authoritative statement, ecclesiastical or otherwise, and this is as it should be. Those few who are looking for a dogmatic pronouncement in favor of premarital intercourse should certainly be denied the immature satisfaction of supposing that this author has settled the issue for them. But, second, it does make *some* difference, and I do not know whether the difference it makes for any particular couple will be for their mutual good or ill.

What I have tried to do is to show what the score is, if the expression can be pardoned. I have argued, in brief, that there is no evidence to show that premarital intercourse is either necessary for a successful marriage or more probable to lead to it, that there are some considerations to show that intercourse is best engaged in within the marriage commitment, but that in certain circumstances exceptions may be justifiable or even beneficial. Whether any individual can or should claim such circumstances, and whether in his case it will prove to be a valid claim, I do not know—and indeed he will not either until long after. Kirkendall concluded that unless the relationship was of long-standing and the couple of more than average maturity premarital intercourse was more likely to be damaging than beneficial.[40] Indeed, he made the striking point that "in practically all instances 'nondamaging' intercourse [a phrase he prefers to the more positive 'strengthening'] occurred in relationships which were already so strong in their own right that intercourse did not have much to offer toward strengthening them." [41]

Here are three considerations which must be weighed before any couple can reasonably conclude that premarital intercourse is likely to be the right solution to their dilemma. First, once moral absolutes are abandoned—as they already are in this field among most students—there is a danger of complete chaos and untold disaster unless those who claim to order their actions by love rather than by law are absolutely honest in examining their motives critically. If it is followed with real integrity, the principle, "love makes it right," will not be less but more demanding than the legalism it has replaced. Second, it is exceptionally difficult to be objective about one's own sexual life. There is no field of human activity in which it is so easy to deceive oneself and to be convinced by arguments which are in fact nothing but rationalizations of clamant desires. Joseph Conrad's dictum, "No man fully understands his own artful dodges to escape from the grim shadow of self-knowledge," is particularly relevant to the sphere of sex. One woman college senior admitted frankly to Gael Greene that "some of us manage to fall in love two or three times a week." [42] And the man who is seriously convinced that intercourse is the appropriate expression of mutual love may in fact be seeking merely to

bolster his own sense of inadequacy or to stifle some inner loneliness. He may only be looking for a mother image or a status symbol. He may be using sex merely as an expression of his power over another person. Finally, the added criterion, "so long as nobody gets hurt," is extremely difficult to apply with any consistency. The decision must surely take account of the effect not only upon the girl and any possible child but also upon the parents and friends and classmates of both parties. I think there may be occasions on which the relative pain caused to others is justified by the much greater benefit to the engaged couple, as in the case cited above (which eventually worked out well). But the private needs of one couple must also be assessed in the light of the possible effect upon society as a whole. To this we shall return after considering a new style of chastity which offers to some students an escape from the dilemma of "to bed or not to bed."

11 EVERYTHING BUT

"I love to make love and if I like a boy, I do. Everything but—, anything but—, whatever you call it. . . . Girls keep telling me that what I am isn't really virginity anymore. You know that line—What's a hymen, anyway, when you've done everything else in the book? But 'that' really is the big step. That's it. And boys do have a habit of bragging, you know. Petting is different. You can have all the warmth and affection and your virginity, too. As long as the boy goes along with you and you both don't get carried away." So one sophisticated coed at a small Eastern college recently propounded her solution to the dilemma of sex.[1] It is a solution widely acclaimed by male students, too, more than half of whom pet to climax,[2] and Kinsey is surely right in stating that a great many engaged couples participate in genital stimulation to orgasm before they marry.[3]

Heavy Petting on the Campus

At the same time, it is the acceptance of heavy petting that most clearly distinguishes the mores of the present student generation from those of their parents and of other educational levels in our society. We have already noted that this divergence accounts for some of the popular misconceptions about sexual excesses on the campus. "Frank and frequent participation in physical stimulation that is openly intended to effect orgasm is definitely more abundant now than it was among older generations," wrote Kinsey.[4] Indeed, some of the practices utilized by young people today are still regarded by many of their parents as abnormal, even within marriage. One-fifth of Kinsey's sample of college-level males, for example, had participated in oral-genital stimulation with a girl outside marriage by the age of twenty-five.[5] The Kronhausens concluded that the "middle-of-the-road majority" of the men they studied accepted mouth-genital contacts, though with a preference for fellatio rather than for cunnilinctus.[6]

It is not surprising, therefore, that some of the older protagonists of sexual freedom view the activities of today's students with undisguised disgust—an interesting illustration of the way in which the revolutionary ideas of one generation become the established orthodoxy of the next. Bertrand Russell, for example, declares that petting and necking without complete intercourse is indicative of perversion.[7] Presumably by the term he means "contrary to nature"; but the widespread assumption that the lower animals never experience orgasm other than in vaginal coitus has been shown to be quite erroneous. Noncoital sex play leading to ejaculation without coitus is observed in other mammals.[8] Mouth-genital contacts are quite common, particularly among anthropoids, and they have been found acceptable in other human societies.[9] Indeed, insofar as the example of the lower animals is relevant (which is not far), it could be argued that the deliberate stimulation of the genitals for the pleasure of the partner is an indication of human maturity, insofar as it represents an other-centered concern and some restraint on mere rutting. Kinsey notes that "the anatomy of the human animal, particularly his hands, may allow him to utilize a wider variety of techniques than most other mammals can use, and the human activity may be more consciously planned, deliberately elaborated, and expertly prolonged." [10]

The Judaeo-Christian religious tradition has condemned petting to climax on the same grounds as it has condemned masturbation. Frequently, indeed, it is categorized as "mutual masturbation." Gael Greene records the very justifiable objection of a Michigan State sophomore to this nomenclature: "I wish they wouldn't call it mutual masturbation. . . . This is a two-people thing and I don't think it is anything we should be ashamed of. We're in love and I feel we show our maturity by limiting ourselves to sexual behavior that can't hurt anyone—as pregnancy would." [11] What is more surprising, however, is the fact that some authorities, who are quite prepared to recognize the useful role played by masturbation in the sexual development of the adolescent, fall into a condemnatory tone when discussing this practice, which certainly has more mutuality and self-giving in it. Phyllis and Eberhard Kronhausen, for example, speak of "the curious kind of morality . . . which a large segment of our college population has adopted," according to which it is more chaste to reach orgasm through manual or oral stimulation of the genitals than through vaginal coitus.[12]

Nevertheless, despite the adult distaste for the modern code, it is precisely our double-faced social mores that have brought heavy petting into such favor as an alternative to coitus. We have started adolescents on the escalator of progressive sexual intimacies, helped to keep their appetites titillated through every available channel, and also impressed upon them, particularly upon the girls, the vital importance of virginity. Understandably, many of them have a profound inner conflict that can only be resolved if some way is found of achieving sexual relief without infringing upon the absolute standard of virginity. At the same time, the market is flooded with books on sexual techniques, both ancient and modern. Although these probably teach very little that is new to any experienced married couple, they do provide the unmarried with suggestions for precoital play, which they very understandably adapt for their own purposes. Through heavy petting, a profound intimacy is achieved, the relief of orgasm is enjoyed, the relationship is maintained in motion, and the threat of pregnancy is avoided. This intimacy, however technical the distinction may seem, definitely does not carry the same sense of guilt, for many, that regular coitus would. Kirkendall noted time and time again that the men he interviewed regarded petting to climax as the natural extension of earlier physical contacts in the relationship.[13] Coitus for most of them, whether they accepted it or not, represented a distinct step. Very few felt any guilt or regret about any type of petting, but many had such reservations after coitus.

Whether the distinction would disappear if our society no longer attached any importance to virginity is irrelevant to the present situation. Personally, I am inclined to think that the integral connection between coitus and marriage suggested in the previous chapter will always mean that there is a quite proper sense of inadequacy and imperfection about engaging in the ultimate intimacy without the ultimate commitment. But whatever the reason—even if it is simply a sense of personal integrity and restraint in maintaining a minimal control over the sexual urge—the avoidance of intercourse clearly has a moral significance for many young men and women today. A Radcliffe student, reported in *Newsweek,* explained, "I used to think it perfect nonsense to lie down with a boy, get undressed, or let him undress me—and then say, 'let's stop.' It's probably bosh, but I have built up this idealistic thing about the final act itself." [14]

It is surely absurd to say that it would be better for a couple to go all the way even if they have strong inhibitions about premarital intercourse. To say, as some do, that virginity is a state of mind, and that, therefore, once a boy and girl have abandoned themselves to each other in intention, there is no point in withholding the final act, does not really help. It is as irrational as it would be to argue that because Jesus said that every man who lusts after a woman has already committed adultery in his heart, it makes no difference whether he goes ahead and commits it with the body. It draws attention to the fact that technical virginity is no matter for self-righteous pride; but it does not alter the fact that something is being preserved for marriage, which, for this particular couple, represents a moral good.

It is equally absurd to expect that a dating pattern which starts with holding hands and kissing good night in the preteens, and progresses steadily through necking, light petting, and deep kissing, can be suddenly halted when some arbitrary boundary is reached, like the frontier in Korea at the thirty-eighth parallel. Indeed, this latter alternative is probably the least desirable, for there is considerable evidence to show that continual stimulation to a point just short of orgasm is likely to be productive of serious nervous disturbance.[15] Ideally, neither premarital intercourse, nor petting to orgasm, is a satisfactory solution to the sexual needs of men and women. But this is no reason for denying that one may be better than the other as a resolution of the dilemma in which the contemporary student finds himself.

Not infrequently, it is suggested that full vaginal coitus is preferable, whatever the hesitations of the couple concerned, because the achievement of orgasm through mutual petting establishes habits which are harmful in marriage, and may make adjustment to regular intercourse difficult. This idea, however, is probably based on the now generally abandoned Freudian distinction between vaginal orgasm and clitoral orgasm in the female.[16] According to this theory, experience in orgasm as a result of manual stimulation of the clitoris can lead to a fixation, as a result of which the woman fails to enjoy orgasm in intercourse. But the facts do not support this theory. Kinsey established that the experience of orgasm in premarital petting is not related to any failure to achieve and enjoy early coital orgasm. Indeed, he concluded that "premarital petting experience contributes definitely to the effectiveness of the sexual relations after marriage," [17] and that petting to orgasm "introduces the female to the physical, psychologic, and social problems that are involved in making emotional adjustments to other individuals." [18] In view of the likelihood, noted in an earlier chapter, that a girl who engages in intercourse without achieving orgasm will have difficulty in making a physical adjustment after marriage, petting to orgasm may offer a more reliable and responsible solution than intercourse, with its attendant risks of guilt feelings or revulsion.[19]

The Promiscuous Virgin

Everything that has been said in this chapter, however, is entirely relative to the quality of the relationship existing between two people. The justification and value of any form of sexual intimacy, whether it be holding hands or kissing, necking or petting, oral-genital stimulation or coitus, depend upon the attitude of the two partners to each other. Where there is no real meeting of the two selves, no elementary sense of mutual response or attraction, even the good-night kiss of a formal date may be entirely inappropriate. Henry Miller, describing an early adolescent mixed party, writes: "Some kissed each other good-bye. The bold ones! Those who lacked the courage to behave with abandon, those who cared, who felt deeply, in other words, were lost in the shuffle. No one noticed their discomfiture." [20] Necking above the waist purely for private pleasure or lust can hardly be defended on any grounds.

But where there is a full and free self-giving commitment, as there should be in marriage, moralists today are generally prepared to grant that no physical stimulation which is mutually acceptable is objectionable or perverse. At what point in the relationship of two people who are not yet married such intimacies as petting to climax or oral-genital contact are appropriate or justifiable, only the mature and responsible couple themselves can decide. In reaching such a decision (and it should, surely, be a decision rather than an unexamined progress), the caveats entered at the conclusion of the last chapter must again be carefully weighed.

But, in addition, the fact must be emphasized that tactile or oral genital stimulation represents, if not the ultimate intimacy, a profound level of physical and sexual union. Divorced from deep and meaningful personal respect and love, it is likely to seem, in the cold light of another day, demeaning and debasing for both parties. The line between these practices and full genital union is real; but it is a very fine one. The man who, out of consideration for his fiancée or because he wishes to reserve the final act for marriage, finds release and mutual comfort in petting, may indeed have found the best available solution. But the man who engages in intimate petting or oral contacts with a casual date, or with a girl for whom he has no concern, is utterly ludicrous if he supposes that thereby he has preserved his or her virginity. The promiscuous virgin, male or female, is far less responsible, less mature, and more generally to be despised than the man who goes all the way with a girl for whom he has real love. Far greater damage and depravity may result from frequent indulgence in noncoital orgasm as a part of superficial sex play than from full coitus as a part of serious courtship. An articulate analysis of this highly complex dilemma, from the girl's point of view, has been made by Gael Greene:

> Technical virginity . . . may not carry the official onus of nonvirginal promiscuity, but it has a similar potential for ugliness and scarring. It becomes an acting out of sex, not an act of love, or even lust. It triggers sordid struggles and shattering hostility in the back seats of automobiles and leafy campus bowers. . . . It can set off fierce self-recrimination, disgust, maiming loss of self-esteem.[21]

The man who seeks to act with integrity will take this challenge to heart before supposing himself relieved of responsibility by his girl's readiness for "everything but—"

12 WHO GETS HURT?

A Columbia University senior who was recently asked whether he favored premarital intercourse replied with another question: "For me—or my kid sister?" [1] He may have been merely reflecting the superficiality of the double standard, which allows a freedom to men that it denies to women. But I think it more likely that he grasped one aspect of the sexual revolution which is very frequently ignored, namely, its long-range effect upon our society. We started this book with a discussion of the schizophrenia of our society and the effect it has upon student thinking about sex. We noted that part of the student's dilemma arises from the fact that his parents have failed to achieve any coherent and honest understanding of sex, and it is obvious that the perpetuation or extension of the present confusion will profoundly affect the following generations. Since most students profess to be concerned with avoiding hurt to others as a result of their sexual freedom, it is impossible, with any consistency, to avoid facing up to the implications of private liberty for the public culture. The immediate and measurable consequences of one unmarried couple sleeping together may be limited to disappointment or disapproval on the part of their parents or friends. The cumulative effect of the widespread acceptance of the practice over the last few decades may ultimately be more significant for our history than the French or Russian revolutions. For, despite the parrotlike repetition of the adage, "What I do with my sex life is my own business," sex is unalterably and inherently social in its ramifications. Unlike some other basic urges, such as hunger, it normally involves another person.

The Implications of the Sexual Revolution

Moreover, it is clear that the sexual standards of our society are changing, and that the change is accelerated when evidence of widespread laxity and irresponsibility is given publicity, as in the Kinsey reports and other studies. Lester Kirkendall, in elaborating on the ideal of interpersonal relationships as the criterion for mature and meaningful sexual intimacy, points out:

A good relationship between two or a few persons is like a stone cast in a pool of water. It creates an ever-widening circle of ripples, which eventually reach the farthest bank. This capacity to extend to and receive acceptance from an ever-expanding world is basic both to the mental health of individuals and to the stability and preservation of a society. . . . Certain experiences may create a closer relationship between two or more persons at a particular time, but how will it work out eventually? [2]

And Gael Greene, reflecting on her interviews with over six hundred students on more than a hundred campuses, came to the conclusion that part of the confusion and inadequacy of their sexual mores was the result of the cult of the individual and the attitude of "to Hell with society," which "seems to cast man off on his own fenced-in island where nothing matters but his own ego and libido." [3]

There is a considerable proportion among the younger generation for whom the disregard of society and any long-term consequences is a conscious assumption. Once again society itself must accept some responsibility for the situation in which it places its junior members. Warren R. Johnson points out that there is a sense of great urgency among many who feel themselves living in the twilight of the human race and are reluctant to be exterminated before they experience sexual love.[4] I am reminded of a conversation between two boys in their early teens which was reported in the London *Times* a few years ago. One asked, "What do you hope to be when you grow up?" And the other replied sadly, "It doesn't matter much because when we're grown up there won't be anything to be grown up on."

For others, of course, it is not the approaching apocalypse that justifies sexual license, but the terrible prospect of adult torpor. You are only young once, so make the most of it before you are sucked into that insipid, lifeless world. "So we must cram all our delinquency into a few brief years before assuming the masks of respectability," argues an English teenager. "Perhaps our generation can beat the inevitable processes of corrosion and corruption, of acceptance and mean acquiescence? Perhaps, perhaps. Meanwhile we fear we might soon regret the things we didn't do while we still had the chance 'of making the best of our youth.' "[5]

Such fears and fantasies are certainly natural, and they appeal to the responsible and thoughtful from time to time as certainly as they obsess the perpetually immature. But a student generation which has shown itself profoundly concerned with such issues as civil rights, poverty, and the Peace Corps is not likely to be permanently blind to the fact that the sexual pattern it chooses is going to have a lot to do with the happiness and character of its kid sisters and its children—not to mention its own future. As V. A. Demant has pointed out, it is only the unscrupulous villain or the completely detached saint who can envisage with equanimity the disintegration of that culture in which he has been nurtured.[6]

Sex and Civilization

The fact is that, in Richard Lewinsohn's words,[7] "man has never been governed exclusively by his loins," and the enticing invitations to sexual anarchy, so vigorously proclaimed by the radical apostles of liberty are in fact an invitation to cultural suicide. Freud recognized that civilization depends for its existence and development upon some restraint of the most urgent sexual drives. He believed that the ego had to mediate between the libidinal impulse to private pleasure and the constructive demands of the group. On some occasion he was reminded that savages make no such choice. And the great man, with typical European arrogance, is reported to have replied, "That is exactly why they are still savages." But more extensive sociological studies have made it clear that even this offensive contrast is unjustified. For, although more primitive races frequently accept sexual practices which seem, by our standards, extremely lax and unrestrictive, they all have some structure of order and discipline. No society that is known accepts complete sexual freedom as a substitute for formal marriage.[8] Moreover, transgressions of the tribal taboos are often punished as severely as they are in the most puritanical Western society.[9]

It remains true, however, as J. D. Unwin has shown, that cultural and intellectual development is related to sexual discipline.[10] He found that societies with more or less complete prenuptial freedom survive only in tribal units. Those requiring some continence before marriage show a more elaborate social system. Those enforcing or requiring premarital continence show the greatest potential for creative social development. Kinsey noted the relevant fact that societies which allow considerable freedom in nonmarital sexual activity are primarily those in which sex is not associated with love and other emotional values.[11] Whatever may have been the errors of medieval asceticism, and however inadequate the church's understanding of human sexuality, the alternative of barbarian license would certainly have been disastrous for the survival of Western culture. "There would have been no modern Europe," says Demant, "if the sexual behaviour of early European man had been as spontaneously unrestricted as that of the natives of Samoa whose sexual freedom so enthrals Margaret Mead." [12] Any student with the most elementary knowledge of Toynbee knows that civilizations are never beyond disintegration, and anyone who has read Toynbee with any care knows that, in his opinion, our civilization is facing a crucial, though not necessarily disastrous, test of its cultural foundations. And in this connection the prophetic warnings of the sociologist Pitirim A. Sorokin cannot be brushed aside. Although Sorokin's analysis may be weighted on the side of pessimism, and his worst fears not yet realized, this was exactly true of the biblical prophets. And it was precisely because their message was dismissed as extravagant that disaster overtook Israel and Judah in turn. Sorokin argues, with impressive documentation, that our culture has replaced its original moral and religious values with purely sensate or secular values over the past centuries, and that these are now in turn disintegrating, with the result that the basic structure by which our society is held together is falling apart:

> The sex drive is now declared to be the most vital mainspring of human behavior. In the name of science, its fullest satisfaction is urged as a necessary condition of man's health and happiness. Sex inhibitions are viewed as the main source of frustrations, mental and physical illness and criminality. Sexual chastity is ridiculed as a prudish superstition. . . . Sexual profligacy and prowess are proudly glamorized. *Homo sapiens* is replaced by *homo sexualis* packed with genital, anal, oral, and cutaneous libidos. . . . Our trend toward sex anarchy has not yet produced catastrophic consequences. Nevertheless, the first syndromes of grave disease have already appeared.[13]

The man who believes that sex is something to be enjoyed at all costs is not going to be troubled by such considerations. But the man who believes that "love makes it right, *so long as nobody gets hurt*" must surely ask himself how his rejection of the standards established in our society will affect its future character.

Kant's principle that one should not do what one is not prepared to see universally done is relevant here. However convinced the student may be of the maturity and soundness of his judgment, he has to consider the background and circumstances which have made this maturity possible. He may be persuaded (perhaps quite rightly) that his private sexual dilemma can best be solved by premarital intercourse. But he has made that deliberate choice against the pressure of family and friends (and perhaps, originally, of the girl), which has forced him to face up to the dangers and disadvantages of the action, and prevented him from rushing headlong into a situation which in many other instances proves disastrous. But suppose that no such public standard had existed. Instead of waiting until he was entirely convinced of his love and permanent commitment to this girl, he might well have gone all the way with several others and endangered both his prospects and theirs for achieving maturity in sexual relationships. He certainly knows dozens of other men, less responsible and considerate, who would have been to bed with many more girls if society raised no barriers—including perhaps his kid sister or his fiancée. Moreover, many of them know it, too, and are in fact relieved that society does not give them carte blanche to follow their unrestrained sexual instincts.

We may be glad that there is not a radar control on every mile of the highway, and most of us occasionally, and some of us for good reasons, break the speed limit. But at the same time if there were no signs to indicate what other travelers had found to be a reasonable speed, most of us would regret it and many of us would be dead. One coed who had been the victim of an entirely permissive upbringing put the point this way:

Kids need restrictions because they don't really understand reasoning. You need a higher thing to judge by. You don't have to say it's "morally right" or "morally wrong"! You can say, it's "unwise" or "safer." Kids understand that. I shall never forgive my parents for never saying "no" to me about anything. It all happened too fast. It would have been better if I'd been 18 instead of 16, if I'd had something to rebel against. I just never realized my parents loved me until recently. I used to think, if they really loved me, they'd care what happened.[14]

It is by no means unknown for students to find that the parietal rules of college administrations, however vigorously deplored in public, provide them with much-needed support and excuse for their better judgment when the pressure toward lower standards is strong and appealing.

The relationship between the individual and society is one of the most controversial and complex questions in any age. When the question is one of material damage, we all recognize that the individual has to limit his freedom in relation to other individuals and to the social order—as, for example, in cases of theft, murder, homicide, or an automobile accident. When the hurt, though less measurable, can be clearly seen to affect specific individuals, most of us recognize the necessity for laws to restrain private license—as in libel, or the exploitation of minors for sexual pleasure. But when it is a matter of more generalized effect, or the accumulative impact of many relatively insignificant individual actions, it becomes far more difficult to defend the common good without doing injustice to the individual. Most of us probably feel that our society has erred in the recent past in its attempts to legislate moral influences and to penalize private offenses against the established standards of sexual propriety. The current revulsion against many of the statutes which attempt to regulate heterosexual or homosexual practice between consenting adults is indicative of this strong change of mind. The widespread dissatisfaction with the rigidity of religious judgments on sexual activities, which is shared by many within the churches, reflects the same trend.

The Need for a Public Ideal

I have made it clear that I sympathize with this revolt against legalism in society and in religion. But I think the reaction is often exaggerated and irrational, and fails to acknowledge that there is an essential place in our society for public standards without which the effects of the sexual revolution may be disastrous. Here are two examples from sources to which we have given considerable attention earlier. Kinsey showed himself well aware of the profoundly religious origins of our social mores.[15] But he does not hide his (often very justified) criticism of the restrictive and irrational approach to sex which has characterized the Judaeo-Christian tradition.[16] Moreover, whenever he refers to the restraints upon sexual outlet which are the result of social or religious prohibitions, it is difficult to avoid the impression that he regards such restraints as either ineffective or in some way undesirable.[17] The public has understandably gained the impression that the norm for healthy sexual life, in Kinsey's view, is the completely free individual satisfaction of whatever animal urge happens to be most pressing.[18] And yet this is not the case. When Kinsey discusses the role of marriage, he recognizes the need for some balance between the individual's desire for coitus with a variety of partners and the social necessity of stability in marriage. But instead of acknowledging that this involves a continuing, and often painful, tension between the individual's sensual satisfaction and his responsibility to the social order (not to mention his wife), Kinsey ducks the issue with the lame statement that this problem "is not likely to be resolved until man moves more completely away from his mammalian ancestry." [19]

The Playboy Philosophy is my second example of an approach to sex which is so mesmerized by the task of crusading against distorted Victorian standards that it fails to offer any effective alternative to private license. "Our view of the world," writes Hugh Hefner, "is predicated on the paramountcy of the individual and each person's inherent individuality. . . . We believe that each individual has a *right* to explore his own individuality—to discover himself, as well as the world around him —and to take pride in himself and the individuality that sets him apart from the rest of mankind." [20] But Hefner is not unaware of the values of society, which, he writes, "should exist not only for the purpose of establishing common areas of agreement among men, but also to aid each person in achieving his own individual identity." [21] He declares himself opposed to impersonal sex when it is "irresponsible, exploitive, coercive, or in some way hurts one of the individuals involved." [22] He assures us that he does not favor an entirely free or permissive attitude toward teenage sex.[23] But he nowhere suggests how such abuses are to be prevented or discouraged unless there is some means whereby society can keep clearly before its members a vital ideal of responsible and mature sexual conduct. Nor does he help his readers, as far as I can tell, to face up to the inevitable conflict between the privilege of exploring one's individual sexuality and the necessary limits that society and maturity will place upon that right. In fact, *Playboy* gives the impression of endorsing more or less uniform promiscuity as the ideal of manliness. Except, of course, for that one qualification which makes it clear that Hefner is neither a libertine nor a competent analyst of the social situation: sex is to be avoided when it "in some way hurts *one of the individuals involved*." But this is an entirely limited view of the effects of sexual activity, which has much wider implications than for the two immediate participants.

It is not any failure to consider the value of the individual person that renders *The Playboy Philosophy* inadequate; it is its failure to take seriously the unavoidable wider social implications of sexual license. Hefner does not, like some, reject all restraints on sexual freedom because he wishes to indulge and have his readers indulge their desires at any cost in human degradation: all honor to him for that. But because of an understandable but groundless fear that any establishment of standards in sexual matters will become oppressive and "puritanical," he has not yet faced up to the fact that the consequences of sexual liberty cannot be restricted to the two individuals involved, and individual freedom must be balanced by corporate judgment and experience. It is worth noting that Boccaccio, whose stories are occasionally retold for the edification of *Playboy* readers, took the view that any kind of treachery or deceit was justified "against a third person (the jealous rival, the parents, or whatever other powers hindered the designs of love), but not against the object of one's love." [24]

The Church and Freedom

Because I shall undoubtedly be accused of reintroducing exactly that legalistic and inflexible spirit against which I protested in the early chapters of this book, I must briefly distinguish what I have in mind from what Kinsey and Hefner and most students fear and repudiate. In the first place, I am not talking about the perpetuation of a legally enforceable code that attempts to regulate the sexual lives of consenting adults. In my opinion the state should concern itself only with those offenses in which criminal force is used, or in which children or the mentally defective are subject to abuse, or in which sexual activity constitutes a public nuisance.[25] But unofficial, independent bodies, which have no power of compulsion or punishment, will always have a vital role to play in upholding responsible sexual behavior. The Christian Church, by its very nature, has an obligation to proclaim the supremacy of love as revealed in Jesus Christ. By its teaching it must challenge the individual to preserve the final intimacy of intercourse for the final commitment of marriage. It must remind men of the complexity of sexual relationships and warn them of the consequences of selfish private indulgence. But it should affirm these standards without denying the freedom necessary for individual judgment and occasional nonconformity. Without compromising on the principle that intercourse should be the expression and seal of the commitment of marriage, the church must make it clear that not all failures to attain the ideal are equally reprehensible. It must reassure the young couple that a decision to compromise with the ideal, because of the realities of twentieth-century life, when honestly and sincerely arrived at, does not cut them off from God's love and grace. It must face the fact that occasionally love requires actions that are outwardly in conflict with what love normally seeks to do. It has to discover some way of upholding ideals without turning them into a rigid law.[26]

But I am not, of course, talking about the kind of sexual ideals with which the churches have been associated in the past. The traditionally negative, repressive, and frequently hypocritical repudiation of sex as a second-best will never again carry weight with informed and educated men; and I have tried to show that it has nothing to do with the life of Jesus, upon whom the churches claim to base their teaching. Nor can the Christian ideal of sex and marriage be any more commended to the world on the basis of arbitrary dogma or with the hidden and quite dishonest sanctions of venereal disease, pregnancy, or imminent nervous disaster. It must be presented, if it is to gain any response, with strict respect for the facts of human experience, and as the conclusion to a full and adequate understanding of man and his nature. This book, it is hoped, will contribute to this task. If the mysteries of sexual relationship are anything like as complex and demanding as I have suggested, I do not think that the churches will lack for men and women sincerely seeking whatever help and grace they can find there to fulfill their true humanity.

Whether the churches will prove capable of meeting such a need, once it is born out of honest and clear thought, rather than imposed by fallacious deduction from uncriticized and unsupported prejudice, I do not know. Ecclesiastical institutions are unconscionably slow to adapt their neat definitions and their oversimplified rules to the realities of human history and new knowledge. Those who find security in established tradition are always fearful that any modification will lead to disintegration. It suits their position to represent the issue in absolute contrasts of black and white, and in this respect they have something in common with the advocates of sexual promiscuity. But, insofar as they prefer to judge the intricacies of sexual behavior by oversimple rules, the churches lack the freedom of Jesus himself. Instead of presenting his followers with another detailed set of regulations, Jesus confronted them with the responsibility of personal decision in the light of the absolute obligation of love —and then assured them that his Father was more interested in the integrity of their response than in the measurement and punishment of their failures. The God of legalism is concerned to keep his hands clean, to uncover evil, and to assign penalties. The God we meet in Jesus Christ runs the risk of associating with prostitutes, refuses to condemn a woman taken in adultery, and welcomes us as we are. The reason why many religious people prefer to worship the God of legalism is that they can claim to exercise the divine prerogative themselves. The follower of Jesus has to accept the more humble role of living as responsibly as he can with the human dilemma, and leaving judgment and forgiveness in the hands of God.

AUTHOR'S NOTES

Chapter 1: Our Double-faced Society

1. Warren R. Johnson, *Human Sex and Sex Education,* p. 32.
2. Reported in *Look* magazine, June 29, 1965, p. 21.
3. *McCall's* magazine, September, 1963, p. 173.
4. *Sex and the College Girl,* p. 87. Hereafter referred to as Greene, *College Girl.*
5. *Ibid.*, p. 29.
6. *Sex Histories of American College Men,* p. 29. Hereafter referred to as Kronhausen, *Histories.* Greene found the same to be true of the girls she interviewed—*College Girl,* p. 164.
7. The best of these is probably *Sex Without Fear,* by S. A. Lewin and John Gilmore pub. by Medical Research Press, 132 West 52 Street, New York, N.Y. 10019.
8. Kronhausen, *Histories,* p. 57.
9. *Sex Without Guilt,* p. 139.
10. Quoted in *The Family and the Sexual Revolution,* ed. by Edwin M. Schur, p. 58.
11. *Saturday Review,* Dec. 12, 1964, pp. 61-62.
12. *Marriage and Morals,* p. 109.
13. *Sexual Behavior in the Human Female,* pp. 298-99. Hereafter referred to as Kinsey, *Female.* Among women born before 1900, only 14 per cent of those still unmarried by 25 had intercourse before marriage. In the generation born between 1900 and 1910, the percentage jumped to 36. Similar figures for the male population were not worked out. However, the incidence of premarital coitus among females is the more significant criterion because the older generation of men made more use of prostitutes, and their *total outlets* did not increase so markedly. The striking change in the percentage of females does not, of course, represent an increase in the number of prostitutes in Kinsey's sample after 1900, but a far greater readiness for "nice" girls to engage in premarital intercourse.
14. Kronhausen, *Histories,* p. 208.
15. The incident and its sequel are described by Hugh M. Hefner in *The Playboy Philosophy* (Chicago: HMH Publishing Co., 1962-65), Part 5. I have used the term "Part" to refer to the original monthly installments, not to the volumes in which these have now been published separately.
16. *Ibid.*
17. Dr. Peter Henderson, reported in *The New York Times,* September, 1963.
18. Quoted by Greene, *College Girl,* p. 209.

Chapter 2: The Student as Scapegoat

1. Pp. 219-22. Hereafter referred to as Kinsey, *Male.* I am not an unqualified admirer of the techniques and assumptions of the Kinsey reports,

but nobody has done a more thorough job, and nobody is likely to do so in the near future. For a sympathetic but critical discussion of the adequacy of the sampling and method adopted by Kinsey, see Seward Hiltner, *Sex Ethics and the Kinsey Reports,* Chap. 3.

2. Italics mine. Dr. Kellogg, whose capacity for making dogmatic pronouncements entirely contrary to the facts is only exceeded by the profundity of his revulsion against all sexuality, is quoted at length in *The Playboy Philosophy,* Part 17, from which this passage is taken.

3. Kinsey, *Male,* p. 222.

4. Kinsey, *Male,* p. 527.

5. Kinsey, *Male,* p. 224.

6. Kinsey, *Male,* p. 264.

7. Kinsey, *Male,* p. 392. Many people dismiss Kinsey's studies, but without producing any alternative statistics. Give or take 10 or even 20 per cent, Kinsey's figures represent a widespread contrast between public morality and private fact. And (whether as a result of Kinsey or not) it is generally agreed that the figures for illicit sexual outlet among students today are considerably higher than they were twenty years ago.

8. "Coming of Age in Great Britain," *The Spectator* (London), May 3, 1963.

9. Pp. 71-72.

10. Vol. 1, No. 1, February, 1965. Information about the Council, which has an outstanding group of officers and board of directors, can be obtained from 1790 Broadway, New York, N.Y. 10019.

11. Kinsey, *Male,* pp. 248-49, 347-48. I have conflated Kinsey's figures for the total male population in the 16-20 (70.5%) and the 21-25 (68.3%) age groups and compared them with those for the 16-20 (41.8%) and 21-25 (53.9%) age groups in the upper educational level.

12. Quoted in *Time* magazine, Jan. 24, 1964, p. 57.

13. Kinsey, *Male,* p. 347.

14. Kinsey, *Male,* p. 351. The exact figure is 28 per cent.

15. Kinsey, *Male,* p. 349.

16. Kinsey, *Male,* p. 552. Italics mine.

17. *Reprise* records, No. 2023; presented by Arthur Cantor.

18. Kinsey, *Male,* pp. 345-46, 377-81.

19. Kinsey, *Male,* p. 609.

20. Kinsey, *Male,* pp. 480-81. Out of a total of 2,102 Protestant and 300 Catholic men between the ages of 16 and 25 in the upper educational level, 850 Protestants and 178 Catholics identified themselves as active or devout.

21. Kinsey, *Male,* pp. 477-79.

22. Apr. 6, 1964.

Chapter 3: The Irrelevance of Religion

1. The value of Goldberg's book is seriously reduced by the absence of specific references and by his overimaginative capacity for finding yonis in everything from horseshoes to figs, and lingams in hot cross buns or walk-

ing canes. Where I am competent to check his use of ancient documents, I find it highly questionable.

2. See Richard Lewinsohn, *A History of Sexual Customs,* pp. 10-11. Hereafter referred to as Lewinsohn, *History.*

3. *The Sacred Fire,* pp. 24-25. Lewinsohn, in the book referred to in the previous note, suggests that love life in the Stone Age was "completely respectable" and not lacking in sensitivity, pp. 12-13.

4. P. 55.

5. *Playboy,* September, 1965, p. 86.

6. Roland Bainton, *Sex, Love, and Marriage,* p. 94.

7. Kinsey, *Male,* pp. 480-81.

8. *Ibid.,* p. 472.

9. The combined figures for devout upper-education-level males engaging in extramarital coitus between 16 and 25 are approximately 1,316 out of 2,952. Kinsey, *Male,* pp. 480-81.

10. Kinsey, *Female,* p. 314. Kinsey regards all such arguments as rationalizations of conscious or unconscious taboos. That they might reflect an innate awareness of the profound significance of sexual intercourse he does not consider.

11. Warren R. Johnson, *Human Sex and Sex Education,* p. 96.

12. Bertrand Russell, for example, can write that Paul "does not suggest for a moment that there may be any positive good in marriage, or that affection between husband and wife may be a beautiful and desirable thing, nor does he take the slightest interest in the family." *Ibid.,* pp. 31-32. Such a caricature of the facts is only made possible by the device of quoting one section of nine verses out of all of St. Paul's letters. See W. G. Cole, *Sex and Love in the Bible,* pp. 156-60.

13. E.g., Gordon Rattray Taylor, *Sex in History.*

14. See V. A. Demant, *Christian Sex Ethics,* pp. 37-38, 97-98.

15. Pp. 232-33. Hereafter referred to as Bailey, *Sexual Relation.*

16. Ephesians 5:22-23.

17. Bailey, *Sexual Relation,* pp. 53-56.

18. P. 3.

19. Ed. by Evelyn M. and Sylvanus M. Duvall.

20. *Ibid.,* p. 51.

21. *Christian Sex Ethics,* p. 38.

22. Bailey, *Sexual Relation,* pp. 56-59.

23. *Ibid.,* pp. 136-37.

24. Quoted in *The New Yorker,* July 25, 1964, with the comment, "So much for the Abelites."

25. Sherwin Bailey, *Sexual Ethics,* p. 48.

26. *Sexual Relation,* p. 208. Bailey argues convincingly that the order of the purposes of marriage (procreation, remedy against sin, mutual society) in the English Book of Common Prayer was not intended by its authors to represent their relative importance. *Ibid.,* pp. 197-99.

27. *The Allegory of Love,* p. 4.

28. See, in addition to the work mentioned in the previous note, Denis

de Rougement, *Love in the Western World*; Robert Briffault, *The Mothers*; A. M. F. Gunn, *The Mirror of Love*; Maurice Valency, *In Praise of Love.*

29. Erich Auerbach, *Mimesis,* p. 198.

30. See Gervaise Mathew, O.P., "Marriage and Amour Courtois in Late Fourteenth Century England," *Essays Presented to Charles Williams* (London: Oxford University Press, 1947).

31. *The Faerie Queene,* proem to Book IV. I owe this reference to my colleague, Professor G. H. Roelofs, who, in an unpublished manuscript, has argued that the customary Platonic interpretation of these lines is inadequate. Certainly, in the *Epithalamion,* Spenser celebrated his own wedding with a description of his wife's beauty which can hardly have been surpassed as an expression of passionate devotion.

32. One of the first books to do so was *The Christian Interpretation of Sex,* by Otto Piper, now revised and reissued as *The Biblical View of Sex and Marriage.*

33. Resolutions 9 and 13, in *The Lambeth Conferences,* 1867-1948 (London: SPCK, 1948), pp. 164-65.

34. *Theology* (London: SPCK), January, 1954, p. 11.

35. As reported in *Newsweek* magazine, Oct. 14, 1963.

36. Pp. 87-89. A lively account of the current debate in Roman Catholic circles is given in *The Pill and Birth Regulation,* ed. by Leo Pyle.

37. H. E. Root, "Ethical Problems of Sex," *God, Sex, and War,* by D. M. MacKinnon and others, pp. 34-35.

38. Kronhausen, *Histories,* p. 224.

39. To be distinguished from *The Playboy Philosophy,* discussed in the next chapter, to which the same description is sometimes applied in the press.

40. *Christian Morals Today,* pp. 13-14, 40-41.

41. *Ibid.,* p. 32.

42. Kinsey, *Female,* p. 260, note 26.

43. Theodor Bovet, *A Handbook to Marriage,* p. 52.

Chapter 4: The Playboy Philosophy

1. The Rev. Roy Larson, quoted in *The Playboy Philosophy,* Part 1.

2. In August, 1965, total sales were 3,000,000 per month, and earlier Starch surveys show that nearly 30 per cent were to men between 18 and 24. *The Playboy Philosophy,* Part 2.

3. According to the Rev. Richard E. Gary, in the *Trialogue* discussion on radio station WINS, New York. *The Playboy Philosophy,* Part 21.

4. *The Playboy Philosophy,* Part 2.

5. The verbatim discussion is reproduced in Parts 19-22 of *The Playboy Philosophy*. The chairman was Murray Burnett, and the other participants were Fr. Norman J. O'Connor, Rabbi Marc H. Tanenbaum, and the Rev. Richard E. Gary.

6. *Ibid.,* Part 16.

7. *Ibid.,* Part 12.

8. *Ibid.,* Part 5.

9. *Ibid.,* Part 7. In Part 3 the animal is referred to as a baby buffalo.

10. *Ibid.*, Part 5.

11. "Toward a New Definition of Obscenity," *Christianity and Crisis*, Jan. 25, 1965.

12. *The Playboy Philosophy*, Parts 7, and 20.

13. The widespread assumption that even blatantly "pornographic" literature is a contributing cause in perversion or delinquency is without substantiating evidence. There are many reputable authorities who believe that it provides an outlet for sexual curiosity which might otherwise lead to seriously antisocial acts. This opinion has been greatly strengthened by the latest report from the Kinsey Institute: *Sex Offenders*, ed. by Paul H. Gebhard. Whether some type of censorship or public discrimination is desirable or workable for children is a moot point. I entirely agree with Hefner that it is absurd to censor adult reading according to juvenile tastes. See *The Playboy Philosophy*, Parts 6, 7, 12, 22. But I think he underestimates the extent to which an early experience of *distorted* sexual literature may make a normal development more difficult. Why should it be argued that the teaching of the church inhibits sexual maturity, but that the worthless vulgarity of, e.g., Terry Southern and Mason Hoffenberg's *Candy* (New York: Putnam, 1964) will be without any such effect on an impressionable child?

14. *The Ethics of Sex*, p. 77.

15. Pp. 199-204. The original appeared in *Christianity and Crisis*, Apr. 17, 1961.

16. *Ibid.*, p. 204.

17. *Time* magazine, Jan. 24, 1964, p. 55.

18. *The Playboy Philosophy*, Part 19.

19. *The Secular City*, pp. 202-3.

20. *The Playboy Philosophy*, Part 1.

21. *The Observer* (London), June 6, 1965.

22. Anthony Storr, *Sexual Deviation*, pp. 9-10.

23. *The Playboy Philosophy*, Part 21.

24. *Ibid.*, Parts 8, 22.

25. Chap. 5.

26. *The Playboy Philosophy*, Part 19.

27. *Playboy*, September, 1965, pp. 87-88.

28. Greene, *College Girl*, pp. 127-30.

29. Kronhausen, *Histories*, pp. 227-28.

Chapter 5: Sex, Lust, and Love

1. *Time* magazine, Jan. 24, 1964, p. 59.

2. Lewinsohn, *History*, p. 62.

3. For a convenient, brief statement of current psychiatric understanding of preadolescent sexuality, I recommend the report *Sex and the College Student*, by the Committee on the College Student of the Group for the Advancement of Psychiatry, which I was privileged to see in manuscript.

4. Douglas Rhymes, *No New Morality*, p .34.

5. Pp. 75-82. One reader of the manuscript of this book complained that I was unfair to Ellis by quoting chiefly from his most superficial book. Al-

though I agree that *Sex and the Single Man* does not do justice to many of Ellis's better insights, and I have referred elsewhere to some of his more solid contributions, I think the criticism irrelevant. The point of view expressed in *Sex and the Single Man* is that which Ellis has elsewhere put forward in popular magazines, and it is certainly widely accepted as the mature conclusion of a qualified expert. Ellis seems to me to have such an irrational revulsion against traditional moral standards that he has become incapable of any adequate assessment of the relative adequacy or inadequacy of different sexual experiences. Thus, he offers us, in *Sex Without Guilt,* a chapter devoted to "The Justification of Sex Without Love."

6. *Ibid.,* p. 81.
7. *Ibid.,* pp. 71-73, 107-8, 232-33.
8. *Ibid.,* p. 30.
9. This identification of love with the negation of life is, however, not really characteristic even of the troubadours. Robert Briffault, in *The Mothers,* has argued convincingly that even the earliest courtly love was passionate and earthy when opportunity offered.
10. V. A. Demant, *Christian Sex Ethics,* p. 45.
11. P. 162.
12. *Sex and the Single Man,* pp. 46-47.
13. *Ibid.,* pp. 93-94.
14. *Ibid.,* p. 47. Italics mine.
15. *The Spectator* (London), May 3, 1963.
16. *Generation X,* ed. by Charles Hamblett and Jane Deverson, p. 77.
17. For a penetrating but, in my opinion, too negative criticism of romantic love, see Seward Hiltner, *Sex Ethics and the Kinsey Reports,* pp. 187-91.
18. *Men, Women, and Marriage,* p. 94.
19. See J. A. T. Robinson, *Honest to God.*
20. *The Secular City,* pp. 259-61. This is not the place to enter upon the question of the *adequacy* of religious language which avoids the word "God," or the usefulness of terms like "the transcendent" as a substitute. I am only arguing here that sexual love may be the *starting point* at which the religious dimension becomes meaningful for today's student.
21. *I and Thou,* Part 3.
22. *Letters and Papers from Prison,* p. 113.
23. *The Playboy Philosophy,* Part 10.
24. Mark 7:21-23.
25. *History,* p. 92.
26. Matthew 5:27-28.
27. In *Gospel and Law,* pp. 18-22.
28. *Christian Morals Today,* pp. 27-29.
29. *The Shaking of the Foundations,* p. 101.
30. John 8:1-11. Although modern scholars are generally agreed that the story did not form part of the original text of the Gospel, it almost certainly records an actual event. That any later Christian would have invented the story is extremely improbable in view of its contrast to later church practice. It could, however, have originated as a dramatic illustration of the saying

that lusting after a woman in the heart involves adultery—those who wish to condemn the woman are obliged to acknowledge that they, too, have been guilty of her sin. But in any case the spirit of the story goes back to Jesus.

31. "Sexuality and Jesus," *The Union Seminary Quarterly Review,* March, 1965, p. 245.

32. *Sexual Deviation,* p. 10.

33. Hebrews 4:15.

Chapter 6: Doing What Comes Naturally

1. Kinsey, *Female,* pp. 448-49; C. S. Ford and F. A. Beach, *Patterns of Sexual Behavior,* pp. 257-58. This statement applies, however, to homosexual acts, not to permanent or exclusive homosexuality, which does appear to be almost unknown in subhuman animals.

2. C. S. Ford and F. A. Beach found that in 64 per cent of the known primitive societies, homosexual activity was acceptable. See *Patterns of Sexual Behavior,* p. 130.

3. Bailey, *Sexual Relation,* pp. 161-62. I am irresistibly reminded of the argument of a recent Archbishop of Canterbury who refused to allow the clergy of the Church of England to marry divorced persons, but welcomed the fact that the state could accommodate them. At the same time, by a most peculiar logic, he persuaded the authorities to put up notices in the secular registrars' offices reminding the couple that marriage is a lifelong commitment. In this way the church sought to impose its standards upon the nation but kept its own hands clean when the system broke down.

4. It is not without significance that Albert Ellis is even today prepared to offer us a "Consumer's Guide to Prostitution," in which he advances once again the pathetic male fallacy that "in our country, at least, girls freely choose to be or not to be harlots, and no one normally forces them to be" (*Sex and the Single Man,* pp. 188-89)—as if that had anything to do with the responsibility of men for the existence of the trade. Since he goes on to advance the myth of the happy, prosperous prostitute, which has been given an additional fillip by the publication of John Cleland's *Fanny Hill* (New York: Putnam, 1963), it may be appropriate to quote Richard Lewinsohn's corrective: "The prostitute's life is a hard and heavy one which ages prematurely those who lead it, blunts the spirit even of the gifted, concentrates their minds on a very restricted sphere of interests, and soon forces them to devote themselves unremittingly to the requirements of their business—the care of their overwrought bodies, their make-up, their little seductive tricks, and the eternal struggle with poverty. There is no time to cultivate the mind, and, as a rule, no need, for the customer does not ask it." (*History,* p. 55.) Even those vigorous defenders of the institution, Harry Benjamin and R. E. L. Masters, in *Prostitution and Morality,* recognize that the prostitute who fails to embark upon an entirely new career (What careers are open?) when her physical charms fail faces the likelihood of a "descent into everincreasing hardship and degradation" (p. 274).

5. Fr. Gregory Baum has indeed argued that this concession makes the

prohibition of birth control by "mechanical" means logically indefensible. See *Christianity and Crisis,* July 26, 1965, p. 162.

6. See Fr. E. C. Messenger, quoted by W. G. Cole, *Sex in Christianity and Psychoanalysis,* p. 144; Theodor Bovet, *A Handbook to Marriage,* p. 96.

7. Kinsey, *Female,* pp. 608-10.

8. Dr. N. Papania, quoted in *The Playboy Philosophy,* Part 17. C. S. Ford and F. A. Beach, in *Patterns of Sexual Behavior,* pp. 251-54, point out that although the evolution from a purely hormonal sexual arousal to the capacity for a largely cerebral arousal is gradual, the latter is strikingly distinctive of man and the higher animals.

9. See Douglas Rhymes, *No New Morality,* pp. 8-14.

10. This point is very vigorously put by several Catholic married couples in the symposium *The Experience of Marriage,* ed. by Michael Novak.

11. Pp. 48-49, 53.

12. *No New Morality,* p. 12.

13. Kinsey, *Male,* pp. 199-203.

14. *Ibid.,* p. 329; cf. also pp. 335, 363 ff., 375 ff.

15. Kinsey, *Female,* pp. 309-10. It is not possible to clear Kinsey of all responsibility for the misuse of his figures, despite these protestations. The reader of his two major works cannot but be aware of a nonscientific, emotional undertone whenever the traditional religious prohibitions on sexual freedom are discussed. A full and sympathetic study is available in *Sex Ethics and the Kinsey Reports,* by Seward Hiltner.

16. *About the Kinsey Report,* ed. by Donald P. Geddes and Enid Curie, p. 17.

17. Kinsey, *Male,* p. 200.

18. *About the Kinsey Report,* ed. by Donald P. Geddes and Enid Curie, p. 63.

19. Kinsey, *Male,* pp. 556-57.

20. *Ibid.,* pp. 549-67. Among those men who never reached grade school, the incidence was 98 per cent; among those whose education stopped at high school, 84 per cent; but among the upper educational group, only 67 per cent.

21. *Ibid.,* p. 351.

22. *Ibid.,* p. 609.

23. Kronhausen, *Histories,* pp. 139, 144.

24. Kinsey, *Male,* pp. 197-205; *Female,* pp. 642-46, 714-61.

25. *The New Republic,* Apr. 4, 1964.

26. *The Playboy Philosophy,* Part 2.

27. *The Playboy Philosophy,* Part 8.

28. *Sex and the Single Man,* p. 14.

29. *About the Kinsey Report,* ed. by Donald P. Geddes and Enid Curie, p. 50.

30. For a clear summary of Freud's ideas, see W. G. Cole, *Sex in Christianity and Psychoanalysis,* Chap. 7.

31. Kinsey, *Male,* p. 207.

32. *Psychology of Sex,* p. 308-9.

33. *Transmutation and Sublimation of Sexual Energies.*

34. *Psychology of Sex,* p. 307.
35. *Psychology of Sex,* p. 221.
36. Kinsey, *Male,* pp. 297-98. On p. 514 Kinsey qualifies this statement as far as it applies to masturbation.
37. *Psychology of Sex,* p. 250.
38. *Reason and Emotion,* quoted by Hugh Montefiore in *God, Sex, and War,* by D. M. MacKinnon and others, p. 76.
39. *Sexual Deviation,* p. 35.
40. *Ibid.,* p. 14.

Chapter 7: Sex—All Alone

1. Kinsey, *Male,* pp. 343-45, 519-25. 99 per cent of all males who go to college have nocturnal emissions, 70 per cent of them before the age of 15. These figures are markedly higher than for the less educated groups, a fact which may be explained by the greater imaginative capacities of students, the paucity of alternative outlets, or their greater reluctance to engage in sexual intercourse before marriage.
2. *Ibid.,* p. 526.
3. Kinsey, *Female,* pp. 192-96.
4. Kinsey, *Male,* p. 508.
5. P. 71.
6. T. Dilworth Harrison, in *Prism* (London), January, 1965. In reply the Rev. Eric James, a previous college chaplain, declared that although he had known young people who had grown in character, and a few who had thrown off the habit, he saw no reason to correlate the two (*ibid.,* May, 1965).
7. Although Kinsey found that many religiously active men masturbated much less frequently than the inactive, 80 per cent of them between the ages of 16 and 25 admitted masturbating at some time. *Male,* pp. 470-73.
8. On this Allan Sherman has commented, "I would like to say, right now, that if they expel all the Boy Scouts of America who masturbate, then next year's Boy Scout Jamboree is going to be a mighty small and lonely affair. . . ." *Playboy,* July, 1965, p. 67.
9. Kinsey, *Male,* p. 513.
10. P. 15.
11. Kinsey, *Male,* p. 514; *Female,* p. 320.
12. *A New Introduction to Moral Theology,* p. 143.
13. Havelock Ellis, *Psychology of Sex,* pp. 92-95.
14. Quoted in *The Playboy Philosophy,* Part 17.
15. W. G. Cole, *Sex in Christianity and Psychoanalysis,* p. 213.
16. *Psychology of Sex,* p. 115.
17. See Frank S. Caprio, *Variations in Sexual Behavior,* Part 1.
18. *Psychology of Sex,* p. 116.
19. Kinsey, *Female,* pp. 390-91. He notes that the correlation may be due to inherent capacities in the women concerned, rather than to cause and effect. Even if this is so, however, there is absolutely no correlation between premarital masturbation and frigidity in Kinsey's findings.
20. See W. B. Pomeroy, "Masturbation—Attitudes and Incidence," *Sex*

Ways in Fact and Faith, ed. by Evelyn M. and Sylvanus M. Duvall, p. 160.

21. G. Hagmaier and R. W. Gleason, *Counselling the Catholic,* pp. 78-79: quoted by W. B. Pomeroy in the chapter referred to in the previous note, p. 156.

22. *A New Introduction to Moral Theology,* p. 143. Waddams does not indeed regard masturbation as a very serious matter, but he does assume that it is in all cases "a sin of overindulgence" (*ibid.,* p. 142).

23. Kronhausen, *Histories,* pp. 87-89.

24. *Homosexuality and the Western Christian Tradition,* p. 163. Hereafter referred to as *Homosexuality.*

25. *Ibid.,* p. 163.

26. *Ibid.,* p. 164.

27. Lewinsohn, *History,* p. 178. Aquinas thereby, as Lewinsohn points out, gave authoritative, though entirely illusory, recognition to the superiority of the male even before birth.

28. *Ibid.,* p. 98.

29. Bailey, *Sexual Relation,* pp. 151-52.

30. Bailey, *Homosexuality,* pp. 99-110.

31. Bailey, *Sexual Relation,* p. 161.

32. See W. G. Cole, *Sex and Love in the Bible,* pp. 297-301.

33. Deuteronomy 14:8 (pork); Exodus 22:18 (witches); Leviticus 20:13 (homosexual acts); Exodus 21:17 (curses); Leviticus 20:18 (menstruation); Leviticus 15:16-17 and Deuteronomy 23:10-11 (wet dreams); Leviticus 15:18 (intercourse).

34. Terry Southern and Mason Hoffenberg, *Candy* (New York: Putnam, 1964), p. 92.

35. *Sexual Deviation,* p. 24.

36. *Psychology of Sex,* pp. 114-15. Albert Ellis dismisses this view as "clap trap" and makes the astonishing statement that "objective observation [whatever that can possibly mean] quickly shows that there are literally millions of people who at least *at times* obtain *more* emotional and physical gratification from masturbation than from any other kind of sex participation [*sic*]." *Sex and the Single Man,* pp. 29-30.

37. Kinsey, *Male,* pp. 541-42; *Female,* p. 263.

38. Most recently in *Prostitution and Morality,* by Harry Benjamin and R. E. L. Masters, p. 279: "What [the prostitute] offers is a release from sexual tension more normal and more satisfying than the relief obtained by masturbation."

39. Kinsey, *Male,* p. 515.

Chapter 8: Sex—All Male

1. Kronhausen, *Histories,* p. 168.

2. P. 29. On the other hand, Donald Webster Cory and John P. LeRoy, in *The Homosexual and His Society* (p. 39), state that anal intercourse is as widely practiced as fellatio among homosexuals, and preferred by many. It is worth remembering that both practices are technically subject to severe penal-

ties in many of the States even when employed by man and wife. See Kinsey, *Female,* p. 370.

3. *Psychology of Sex,* p. 295.

4. "Homosexuality and the Mystique of the Gigantic Penis," *Homosexuality, Its Causes and Cure,* by Albert Ellis, pp. 278-79. See also Chap. 6 of *The Homosexual and His Society,* Donald Webster Cory and John P. LeRoy.

5. See D. J. West, *Homosexuality,* p. 47; Kinsey, *Male,* pp. 613-15.

6. Peter Bruitenhuis, *The New York Times Book Review,* June 30, 1963.

7. P. 167.

8. *Homosexuality,* pp. 41, 56.

9. Quoted in *The Playboy Philosophy,* Part 16.

10. *The New York Times Week in Review,* May 30, 1965, p. E5. The *Times* drew attention to the fact that a speech for the bill in the Lords was made by the great-grandson of the Marquess of Salisbury, who in 1895 initiated the proceedings which sent Oscar Wilde to prison for homosexual conduct.

11. *Ibid.,* p. E12.

12. Sherwin Bailey, *Homosexuality,* pp. 79, 98-99, 140.

13. *Ibid.,* p. 27.

14. *Ibid.,* p. 28.

15. *Canterbury Diocesan Notes* (England), November, 1953.

16. Sherwin Bailey, *Homosexuality,* pp. 38-40.

17. Romans 1:27; I Timothy 1:9-10.

18. *Towards a Quaker View of Sex,* p. 27.

19. *Prism* (London), May, 1965, p. 50.

20. *Homosexuality,* pp. 164-65. In an essay in *They Stand Apart,* ed. by J. T. Rees and H. V. Usill, Bailey distinguishes between the (material) sinfulness and the blameworthiness of homosexual acts; but bases the distinction entirely upon the individual's sense of guilt, and surprisingly ignores the relevance of the quality of the relationship expressed.

21. In an editorial, Feb. 23, 1963.

22. P. 36.

23. *Ibid.,* p. 21. But elsewhere, quite inconsistently, the group does recognize that homosexual relationships "can never give true satisfaction" (p. 34).

24. *Psychology of Sex,* pp. 217-19.

25. In *Homosexuality, Its Causes and Cure,* by Albert Ellis, p. 279. Italics mine. In *The Homosexual and His Society* (Chap. 3), Donald Webster Cory appears to accept this dichotomy without too much concern. But the total divorce of sex from true human relationship is precisely the tragedy of the homosexual, and exactly what the responsible man cannot accept.

26. *The Sixth Man,* p. 14.

27. *Male,* pp. 413-14.

28. For a thoughtful discussion of this question, see Donald Webster Cory and John P. LeRoy, *The Homosexual and His Society,* Chap. 16.

29. D. J. West, *Homosexuality,* p. 52.

30. Quoted in *The Sixth Man,* pp. 160-61.
31. *City of Night,* p. 159.
32. Those who argue that bisexuality or ambisexuality is the norm do not by this justify the assumption that *exclusive* homosexuality is natural to the human species. See *Sexual Inversion,* ed. by Judd Marmor, p. 11 and Chap. 2.
33. Donald Webster Cory and John P. LeRoy, *The Homosexual and His Society,* p. 15.
34. Evelyn Hooke, "Male Homosexuals and their 'Worlds,'" *Sexual Inversion,* ed. by Judd Marmor, pp. 93-97. The same is not true of Lesbians, who frequently establish long-standing relationships involving deeper personal loyalty and love.
35. Albert Ellis, *Homosexuality, Its Causes and Cure,* p. 279.
36. *Sexual Deviation,* p. 89.
37. Donald Webster Cory and John P. LeRoy, *The Homosexual and His Society,* p. 14.
38. *Homosexuality,* p. 55.
39. *The Sixth Man,* p. 13.
40. *City of Night,* p. 85.
41. *Homosexuality,* p. 169.
42. *Male,* pp. 647, 650.
43. *Ibid.,* p. 664.
44. *Ibid.,* pp. 616-17.
45. *Ibid.,* pp. 650-51.
46. *Homosexuality: Disease or Way of Life?,* p. 168.
47. D. J. West, *Homosexuality,* pp. 29-31.
48. The figures are approximate, and are deduced from charts and tables on pp. 170, 630, and 643 of Kinsey, *Male.*
49. Quoted by D. J. West, *Homosexuality,* p. 31.
50. *Histories,* pp. 169, 185.
51. *Psychology of Sex,* p. 204.
52. *Homosexuality,* pp. 162-63.
53. A full summary of the evidence is provided in *Homosexuality, Its Causes and Cure,* Chap. 1, by Albert Ellis. Since I have taken issue with Ellis on other questions, I am glad to be able to commend this study.
54. *Homosexuality,* p. 133.
55. *Sexual Inversion,* ed. by Judd Marmor, p. 10.
56. See Peter Mayerson and Harold I. Lief, "Psychotherapy of Homosexuals," *Sexual Inversion,* ed. by Judd Marmor, Chap. 17.

Chapter 9: The Girl's Point of View

1. *Female,* p. 688.
2. *Ibid.,* pp. 164, 384-85.
3. *Ibid.,* Chap. 14.
4. P. 13 above.
5. *Female,* pp. 125-26. Whereas 92 per cent of the male population has achieved orgasm by the age of 15, the corresponding figure for women is less

than 25 per cent; and the female population does not reach the accumulative incidence of 92 per cent until the age of 29. *Male,* p. 187.

6. *Female,* pp. 626-27
7. *Ibid.,* pp. 649-89.
8. *Ibid.,* pp. 660, 669-70.
9. *Ibid.,* p. 122.
10. *Ibid.,* p. 125.
11. "Some females who at times have high rates of outlet may go for weeks or months or even years with very little outlet, or none at all. But then after such a period of inactivity the high rates of outlet may develop again. Discontinuities in total outlet are practically unknown in the histories of males." *Ibid.,* pp. 681-82.
12. *Ibid.,* p. 352.
13. *Men, Women, and Marriage,* p. 30.
14. *Ibid.,* p. 44.
15. Harry A. Williams, "Theology and Self-Awareness," *Soundings,* ed. by Alec R. Vidler, pp. 81-82.
16. *Sexual Deviation,* p. 31.
17. Introduction to Dante's *Divine Comedy,* Part II: Purgatory (Baltimore: Penguin Classics, 1955), p. 33. I owe the quotation to V. A. Demant, *Christian Sex Ethics,* p. 87.
18. *College Girl,* p. 95.
19. *Ibid.,* pp. 153-54.
20. "How Young Men Influence the Girls Who Love Them," *Redbook* magazine, July, 1965.
21. *Sex and the Single Girl,* p. 23.
22. Kinsey, *Male,* p. 364; *Female,* p. 314.
23. *Male,* p. 589.
24. Greene, *College Girl,* pp. 126-30.
25. *Premarital Intercourse and Interpersonal Relationships,* pp. 64, 88-89, 114, 119, 137. Hereafter referred to as *Premarital Intercourse.*
26. In an address to the tenth annual meeting of the Academy of Psychosomatic Medicine, October, 1963. Printed in *The Western Journal of Surgery, Obstetrics, and Gynecology,* November-December, 1963.
27. Introduction to *Sex and the College Girl,* p. 6.
28. *Reprise* records, No. 2023; presented by Arthur Cantor.
29. Quoted in *Generation X,* ed. by Charles Hamblett and Jane Deverson, p. 32.
30. *Histories,* pp. 212-13.
31. *Female,* p. 316. Kirkendall (*Premarital Intercourse,* p. 206) suggests that "no regrets" is a very negative standard by which to measure the value of premarital intercourse, and might be affirmed by a person with little or no concern other than for private satisfaction.
32. "How Young Men Influence the Girls Who Love Them," *Redbook* magazine, July, 1965.
33. Kirkendall, *Premarital Intercourse,* pp. 127-28, 163-64.
34. *College Girl,* p. 185.

Chapter 10: Love Makes It Right

1. Kronhausen, *Histories,* pp. 139-48; *Premarital Intercourse,* pp. 50-52. The argument of Harry Benjamin and R. E. L. Masters, *Prostitution and Morality,* pp. 197-200, that the fault lies in inadequate sex education is completely speculative.
2. Kirkendall, *Premarital Intercourse,* pp. 80-81, 112-14.
3. Kirkendall, *Ibid.,* p. 155, found that over half the men who had engaged in coitus with a girl to whom they felt considerable attachment had later regrets about the act.
4. Kronhausen, *Histories,* p. 228.
5. Kirkendall, *Premarital Intercourse,* pp. 199-200.
6. *Female,* p. 327.
7. *The New York Times,* Sept. 5, 1965, p. 10E.
8. *Saturday Review,* Dec. 12, 1964, p. 61.
9. *College Girl,* pp. 89, 93, 165, 172.
10. *Ibid.,* pp. 168-69.
11. *Ibid.,* p. 166.
12. P. H. Gebhard, W. B. Pomeroy, C. E. Martin, and C. V. Christenson, *Pregnancy, Birth, and Abortion,* p. 46.
13. *Time* magazine, Jan. 24, 1964, p. 58.
14. *Pregnancy, Birth, and Abortion,* pp. 199-202. *Per Contra,* see Warren R. Johnson, *Human Sex and Sex Education,* p. 46.
15. *Ibid.,* pp. 205, 208-11.
16. *College Girl,* p. 191.
17. *Histories,* p. 134.
18. *Sex and the Single Girl,* p. 28.
19. P. 29.
20. *Playboy,* September, 1965, p. 86.
21. *Female,* pp. 328-30.
22. *Female,* pp. 125-26.
23. *Female,* p. 329.
24. Quoted by Kirkendall, *Premarital Intercourse,* p. 205.
25. P. 370.
26. *Ibid.,* pp. 387-88. Italics mine. For the moral and religious hesitations involved, see *ibid.,* p. 306.
27. *Ibid.,* pp. 427-28.
28. *Ibid.,* p. 428.
29. *Premarital Intercourse,* pp. 178, 169-70.
30. *Ibid.,* pp. 162-64, 170-74.
31. *Male,* p. 364; *Female,* p. 323.
32. Quoted by Greene, *College Girl,* p. 147.
33. *Male,* p. 561.
34. *The Biblical View of Sex and Marriage,* p. 35.
35. *The Christian Man,* pp. 60-61. A summary of Hamilton's position, in *Christianity and Crisis,* greatly helped me in my own thinking, and the pres-

ent chapter undoubtedly reflects other facets of his approach to the subject.

36. *The Mystery of Love and Marriage,* p. 53.
37. *Ibid.,* pp. 53-54.
38. *Premarital Intercourse,* pp. 190-92.
39. *Ibid.,* pp. 166-67.
40. *Ibid.,* pp. 194-95.
41. *Ibid.,* pp. 199-200.
42. *College Girl,* p. 100.

Chapter 11: Everything But

1. Quoted by Greene, *College Girl,* p. 125.
2. Kinsey, *Male,* p. 536-37.
3. *Ibid.,* p. 540.
4. *Ibid.,* p. 245.
5. *Ibid.,* p. 370. The statement in *The Playboy Philosophy,* Part 16, that the percentage of oral-genital contacts rises to 72 among the college group is true but misleading. That figure is reached only in the 36 to 40 age group and includes premarital, marital, and homosexual experiences.
6. *Histories,* p. 258.
7. *Marriage and Morals,* p. 107.
8. Kinsey, *Female,* pp. 229-30.
9. Kinsey, *Male,* p. 371.
10. *Female,* p. 230.
11. *College Girl,* p. 116.
12. *Histories,* p. 239.
13. *Premarital Intercourse,* p. 168.
14. Apr. 4, 1964, p. 54.
15. Kinsey, *Male,* pp. 541-42; *Female,* p. 263.
16. Kinsey, *Female,* pp. 579-84. Kinsey found that hundreds of the women he interviewed suffered from considerable anxiety over the failure to accomplish the biological impossibility of an orgasm centering in the relatively insensitive vagina.
17. *Male,* p. 546.
18. *Female,* pp. 265-66.
19. P. 133 above.
20. *The World of Sex,* p. 38.
21. *College Girl,* p. 120.

Chapter 12: Who Gets Hurt?

1. "The Morals Revolution on the U.S. Campus," *Newsweek* magazine, Apr. 6, 1964.
2. *Premarital Intercourse,* pp. 7-8.
3. *College Girl,* pp. 38-39.
4. *Human Sex and Sex Education,* p. 54.
5. Quoted in *Generation X,* p. 36.
6. *Christian Sex Ethics,* p. 94.

7. *A History of Sexual Customs,* p. 21.
8. Kinsey, *Female,* p. 413.
9. See C. S. Ford and F. A. Beach, *Patterns of Sexual Behavior,* pp. 180-84.
10. *Sex and Culture.* Summarized by V. A. Demant, *Christian Sex Ethics,* pp. 100-101.
11. *Female,* p. 413.
12. *Christian Sex Ethics,* p. 38.
13. "The American Sex Revolution," *The Family and the Sexual Revolution,* ed. by Edwin M. Schur, pp. 151-53.
14. Quoted by Greene, *College Girl,* p. 208.
15. *Male,* pp. 465-68.
16. E.g., *Male,* pp. 472-76 (masturbation); *Female,* pp. 259-61 (petting); *Male,* p. 571 (premarital relations).
17. E.g., *Male,* pp. 477, 549, 589.
18. E.g., especially *Male,* Chap. 6, with its repudiation of any possibility of "sublimation."
19. *Female,* p. 436.
20. *The Playboy Philosophy,* Part 13.
21. *Ibid.*
22. *Ibid.,* Part 19.
23. *Ibid.,* Part 21.
24. Erich Auerbach, *Mimesis,* p. 198. I owe the point to my colleague, the Rev. Donald Rogan.
25. These are basically the criteria proposed by the American Law Institute; the Group for the Advancement of Psychiatry; and the Institute for Sex Research, in its latest volume, *Sex Offenders,* ed. by Paul H. Gebhard.
26. What I am speaking about is, of course, the perennial problem of the relation of gospel and law in theology. I prefer to avoid these terms because they are either unintelligible or seriously misleading to the average reader. But those Episcopalians and others who find it difficult to justify exceptions to ecclesiastical law may find it comforting to remember that the principle of "economy" has long served this purpose in the Orthodox churches.

BIBLIOGRAPHY

Assagioli, Roberto. *Transmutation and Sublimation of Sexual Energies.* New York: Psychosynthesis Research Foundation, 1963.

Auerbach, Erich. *Mimesis.* New York: Doubleday, Anchor Book, 1957.

Bailey, Derrick Sherwin. *Homosexuality and the Western Christian Tradition.* London: Longmans, Green, 1955.

——— *Sexual Ethics.* New York: Macmillan, 1962, 1963.

——— *Sexual Relation in Christian Thought.* New York: Harper & Row, 1959.

——— *The Mystery of Love and Marriage.* New York: Harper & Row, 1952.

Bainton, Roland H. *Sex, Love, and Marriage.* New York: Association Press, 1957.

Benjamin, Harry, and Masters, R. E. L. *Prostitution and Morality.* New York: Julian Press, 1964.

Bergler, Edmund. *Homosexuality: Disease or Way of Life?* New York: Crowell-Collier, 1962.

Bonhoeffer, Dietrich. *Letters and Papers from Prison* (paperback). New York: Macmillan, 1962.

Bovet, Theodor. *A Handbook to Marriage.* New York: Doubleday, Dolphin Book, 1958.

Briffault, Robert. *The Mothers.* New York: Grosset & Dunlap, Universal Library, 1963.

Brown, Helen Gurley. *Sex and the Single Girl.* New York: Bernard Geis, 1962.

Buber, Martin. *I and Thou.* New York: Scribners, 1958, 2nd Ed.

Burgess, E. W., and Wallin, P. *Engagement and Marriage.* Philadelphia: Lippincott, 1953.

Caprio, Frank S. *Variations in Sexual Behavior.* New York: Citadel Press, 1955.

Cole, William Graham, *Sex and Love in the Bible.* New York: Association Press, 1959.

——— *Sex in Christianity and Psychoanalysis.* New York: Oxford University Press, 1955.

Cory, Donald Webster, and LeRoy, John P. *The Homosexual and His Society.* New York: Citadel Press, 1963.

Cox, Harvey. *The Secular City.* New York: Macmillan, 1965.

Demant, V. A. *Christian Sex Ethics.* New York: Harper & Row, 1964.

Dodd, C. H. *Gospel and Law.* New York: Columbia University Press, 1951.

Duvall, Evelyn M. and Sylvanus M. (eds.) *Sex Ways in Fact and Faith.* New York: Association Press, 1961.

Ellis, Albert. *Homosexuality: Its Causes and Cure.* New York: Lyle Stuart, 1965.

——— *Sex and the Single Man*. New York: Lyle Stuart, 1963.
——— *Sex Without Guilt*. New York: Lyle Stuart, 1958.
Ellis, Havelock. *Psychology of Sex*. London: Pan Books, 1959 (originally 1933).

Ford, C. S., and Beach, F. A. *Patterns of Sexual Behavior*. New York: Harper & Row, 1951.
Fryer, Peter. *Mrs. Grundy*. New York: London House & Maxwell, 1964.

Gebhard, P. H., Pomeroy, W. B., Martin, C. E., and Christenson, C. V. *Pregnancy, Birth, and Abortion*. New York: Harper & Row, 1958.
Gebhard, Paul H. (ed.) *Sex Offenders*. New York: Harper & Row, 1965.
Geddes, Donald P., and Curie, Enid. (eds.) *About the Kinsey Report*. New York: New American Library, Signet Book, 1948.
Goldberg, B. Z. *The Sacred Fire*. New York: Grove Press, 1962.
Gover, Robert. *The One Hundred Dollar Misunderstanding*. New York: Grove Press, 1962.
Greene, Gael. *Sex and the College Girl*. New York: Dell, 1964.
Group for the Advancement of Psychiatry. *Sex and the College Student*. New York: 1965.
Gunn, A. M. F. *The Mirror of Love*. Lubbock: Texas Technological Press, 1952.

Hagmaier, G., and Gleason, R. W. *Counselling the Catholic*. New York: Sheed & Ward, 1959.
Hamblett, Charles, and Deverson, Jane. *Generation X*. London: Tandem Books, 1964.
Hamblin, Robert L., and Blood, Robert O., "Premarital Experience and the Wife's Sexual Adjustment," *Social Problems*, October, 1956.
Hamilton, William. *The Christian Man*. Philadelphia: Westminster Press, 1956.
Havemann, Ernest. *Men, Women, and Marriage*. New York: Doubleday & Company, 1962.
Hefner, Hugh M. *The Playboy Philosophy*. Chicago: HMH Publishing Co., 1962-65. In references throughout this book, the term "Part" refers to the original monthly installment, not to the volumes in which many of these have now been republished. Unfortunately, the volumes are without page numbers.
Heron, Alastair. (ed.) *Towards a Quaker View of Sex*. London: Friends Home Service Committee, 1963.
Hiltner, Seward. *Sex Ethics and the Kinsey Reports*. New York: Association Press, 1953.

Johnson, Warren R. *Human Sex and Sex Education*. Philadelphia: Lea & Febiger, 1963.

Kazantzakis, Nikos. *The Last Temptation of Christ.* New York: Simon & Schuster, 1960.

Kinsey, A. C., Pomeroy, W. B., and Martin, C. E. *Sexual Behavior in the Human Male.* Philadelphia: Saunders, 1948.

Kinsey, A. C., Pomeroy, W. B., Martin, C. E., and Gebhard, P. H. *Sexual Behavior in the Human Female.* Philadelphia: Saunders, 1953.

Kirkendall, Lester A. *Premarital Intercourse and Interpersonal Relationships.* New York: Julian Press, 1961.

———*Sex Education* (SIECUS Discussion Guide No. 1). New York: SIECUS (1790 Broadway, 11019), 1965.

Krafft-Ebing, Richard von. *Psychopathia Sexualis.* New York: Putnam, 1965.

Kronhausen, Phyllis and Eberhard. *Sex Histories of American College Men.* New York: Ballantine Books, 1960.

Lewin, S. A., and Gilmore, John. *Sex Without Fear.* New York: Medical Research Press, 1962, rev. ed.

Lewinsohn, Richard. *A History of Sexual Customs.* New York: Premier Books, 1961.

Lewis, C. S. *The Allegory of Love.* London: Oxford University Press, 1938, corrected ed.

——— *The Screwtape Letters.* New York: Macmillan, 1943.

MacKinnon, D. M., and others. *God, Sex, and War.* Philadelphia: Westminster Press, 1965

MacKinnon, D. M., and others. *Objections to Christian Belief.* Philadelphia: Lippincott, 1964.

Macmurray, John. *Reason and Emotion.* New York: Barnes & Noble, 1962.

Marmor, Judd. (ed.) *Sexual Inversion.* New York: Basic Books, 1965.

McCarthy, Mary. *The Group.* New York: New American Library, Signet Book, 1964.

Miller, Henry. *The World of Sex.* New York: Grove Press, 1965.

Novak, Michael. (ed.) *The Experience of Marriage.* New York: Macmillan, 1964.

Piper, Otto. *The Biblical View of Sex and Marriage.* New York: Scribners, 1960.

Pyle, Leo. (ed.) *The Pill and Birth Regulation.* Baltimore: Helicon Press, 1964.

Rechy, John. *City of Night.* New York: Grove Press, 1963.

Rees, J. T., and Usill, H. V. (eds.) *They Stand Apart.* New York: Macmillan, 1955.

Rhymes, Douglas. *No New Morality.* London: Constable, 1964.

Roberts, Thomas D., and others. *Contraception and Holiness.* New York: Herder & Herder, 1964.

Robinson, J. A. T. *Christian Morals Today.* Philadelphia: Westminster Press, 1964.

——— *Honest to God.* Philadelphia: Westminster Press, 1963.

Rougement, Denis de. *Love in the Western World.* New York: Pantheon Books, 1956.

Rubin, Isadore. *Homosexuality* (SIECUS Discussion Guide No. 2). New York: SIECUS (1790 Broadway, 10019), 1965.

Russell, Bertrand. *Marriage and Morals.* New York: Bantam Books, 1959 (originally 1929)

Sayers, Dorothy L. *The Other Six Deadly Sins.* London: Methuen, 1943.

Schur, Edwin M. (ed.) *The Family and the Sexual Revolution.* Bloomington: Indiana University Press, 1964.

Solovyov, Vladimir. *A Solovyov Anthology,* ed. by S. L. Frank. London: SCM Press, 1950.

Stearn, Jess. *The Sixth Man.* New York: Macfadden-Bartell, 1962.

Storr, Anthony. *Sexual Deviation.* Baltimore: Penguin Books, 1964.

Taylor, Gordon Rattray. *Sex in History.* New York: Vanguard Press, 1954.

Thielicke, Helmut. *The Ethics of Sex.* New York: Harper & Row, 1964.

Tillich, Paul. *The Shaking of the Foundations.* New York: Scribners, 1948.

Unwin, J. D. *Sex and Culture.* London: Oxford University Press, 1934.

Valency, Maurice. *In Praise of Love.* New York: Macmillan, 1959.

Vidler, Alec R. (ed.) *Soundings.* London: Cambridge University Press, 1962.

Waddams, Herbert. *A New Introduction to Moral Theology.* New York: Seabury Press, 1965.

West, Donald J. *Homosexuality.* London: Penguin Books, 1960.

Wood, Robert W. *Christ and the Homosexual.* New York: Vantage Books, 1960.

ACKNOWLEDGMENTS

Grateful acknowledgment is made to the following publishers for permission to use copyrighted material from the titles listed below:

Ballantine Books, Inc.—Phyllis and Eberhard Kronhausen, *Sex Histories of American College Men.* Copyright © 1960 by Eberhard Kronhausen.

The Bobbs-Merrill Company, Inc.—Douglas Rhymes, *No New Morality.* Copyright © 1964 by Douglas Rhymes; reprinted by permission of the publishers.

Christianity and Crisis, Inc.—Howard Moody, "Toward a New Definition of Obscenity," January 25, 1965, issue of *Christianity and Crisis.* Copyright © 1965 by Christianity and Crisis, Inc.

Delacorte Press—Max Lerner, "Introduction," in *Sex and the College Girl,* by Gael Greene.

Doubleday & Company, Inc.—Ernest Havemann, *Men, Women, and Marriage.*

Friends Home Service Committee—Alastair Heron, ed., *Towards a Quaker View of Sex.*

Grove Press, Inc.—John Rechy, *City of Night.* Copyright © 1963. Robert Gover, *One Hundred Dollar Misunderstanding.* Copyright © 1961 by Robert Gover.

Harper & Row, Publishers, Inc.—Derrick Sherwin Bailey, *Sexual Relation in Christian Thought.* Used by permission.

William Heinemann Medical Books, Ltd., and Pan Books, Ltd.—Havelock Ellis, *Psychology of Sex.* Used by permission of the publishers.

Herder and Herder—Rosemary Ruether's essay in *Contraception and Holiness,* ed. by Thomas D. Roberts. Copyright © 1964 by Herder and Herder, Inc.

HMH Publishing Company—Hugh M. Hefner, "The Playboy Philosophy," in *Playboy* Magazine. Copyright © 1963, 1964, 1965 by HMH Publishing Company.

Indiana University Press—Edwin M. Schur, ed., *The Family and the Sexual Revolution.* Copyright © 1964 and used by permission of Indiana University Press.

Institute for Sex Research, Inc.—A. C. Kinsey, W. B. Pomeroy, C. E. Martin, and P. H. Gebhard, *Sexual Behavior in the Human Female.* Copyright © 1953 by W. B. Saunders Company. A. C. Kinsey, W. B. Pomeroy, and C. E. Martin, *Sexual Behavior in the Human Male.* Copyright © 1948 by W. B. Saunders Company.

The Julian Press, Inc.—Lester A. Kirkendall, *Premarital Intercourse and Interpersonal Relationships.* Copyright © 1961 and used by permission of The Julian Press, Inc.

J. B. Lippincott Company—H. A. Williams, "Psychological Objections," in *Objections to Christian Belief,* by D. M. MacKinnon, *et al.* Copyright © 1963 by H. A. Williams.

The Macmillan Company—Harvey Cox, *The Secular City.* Copyright © 1965.

McCall Corporation—Mary Calderone, "How Young Men Influence the Girls Who Love Them," in *Redbook* Magazine, July, 1965. Used by permission of McCall Corporation and *Redbook* Magazine.

Methuen & Company, Ltd.—Dorothy L. Sayers, *The Other Six Deadly Sins.* Copyright © 1943 by Methuen & Company, Inc., London. Used by permission of A. Watkins, Inc., agents for Dorothy L. Sayers Estate.

The New American Library, Inc.—Donald P. Geddes and Enid Curie, eds., *About the Kinsey Report*. Copyright © 1948 by The New American Library, Inc.

The New Republic—Christopher Jencks's review of "Sex and the College Girl," in *The New Republic,* April 4, 1964. Used by permission of The New Republic, Copyright © 1964 by Harrison-Blaine of New Jersey, Inc.

Penguin Books, Ltd.—Anthony Storr, *Sexual Deviation*. Used by permission of Penguin Books, Ltd.

SCM Press, Ltd.—Vladimir Solovyov, "The Meaning of Love," in *A Solovyov Anthology,* arranged by S. L. Frank. Copyright © 1950 by SCM Press, London.

Charles Scribner's Sons—Paul Tillich, *The Shaking of the Foundations*. Copyright © 1948 by Charles Scribner's Sons.

The Spectator, London—Colin MacInnes's article in *The Spectator,* May 3, 1963, issue. Used by permission.

Lyle Stuart, Publisher—Albert Ellis, *Sex Without Guilt*. Used by permission of Lyle Stuart. Copyright © 1958.

Tandem Books, Ltd.—Charles Hamblett and Jane Deverson, *Generation X*. Copyright © 1964 by Tandem Books, Ltd., London.

Union Theological Seminary—Tom F. Driver, "Sexuality and Jesus," in the *Union Seminary Quarterly Review,* March, 1965. Copyright © 1965 by Union Theological Seminary in the City of New York. Quoted by permission of the author.

The Westminster Press—William Hamilton, *The Christian Man*. Copyright © 1956 by W. L. Jenkins. Used by permission of The Westminster Press. John A. T. Robinson, *Christian Morals Today*. Copyright © 1964 by SCM Press, Ltd. Published U.S.A. 1964 by The Westminster Press. Used by permission. H. E. Root, "Ethical Problems of Sex," in *God, Sex, and War*. From © Ethical Problems of Sex, H. E. Root, 1963.

My debt to my wife, Mary, is incalculable. She read the manuscript, suggested the title, and looked after four demanding children, virtually single-handed, through a long summer while I worked on the book. Many others have read parts of the manuscript, and I am particularly grateful to the following for criticisms and suggestions: Professor Robert Burns, Dr. Mary S. Calderone, Professor Alden Kelley, President F. Edward Lund, Professor Hayden McCallum, Mrs. Robert Page, Mrs. Gerrit Roelofs, the Reverend Donald Rogan, Dr. Isadore Rubin, and the Reverend Richard Stott. Mrs. Lewis Haldeman, Mrs. John Lincoln, and Mrs. Glenn Mayer gave unsparingly of their time in typing the manuscript at different stages.

INDEX